# SOFT FURNISHINGS
# FOR YOUR HOME

**Golden Hands Books**

Marshall Cavendish
London and New York

**Picture Credits**
J. Ahlberg 87
Malcolm Aird 23, 38
Simon Scott Brown 7, 49
Camera Press 17, 28, 29, 35
59 (Jacques Hartz) 80, 81
Frances Ross Duncan 23, 53
D.M.C. 37, 86
Suzanne Ives 8, 9, 25, 67, 68, 69
Chris Lewis 51
Josephine Rankin 71
Paul Redman 47, 64, 79
Peter Watkins 73
Paul Williams 41

**Edited by** Yvonne Deutch and Sue Simmons

Published by
Marshall Cavendish Publications Limited,
58 Old Compton Street
London W.1V 5PA

© Marshall Cavendish Limited,
1971/1972/1973/1974/1975

This material was first published by
Marshall Cavendish Limited
in the partwork *Golden Hands*

This volume published 1975

Printed in Great Britain by
Ben Johnson & Company Limited
ISBN 085685 095 0

This volume is not to be sold in
the U.S.A., Canada and the Philippines

# Introduction

The most effective way to completely transform your home is by the clever use of soft furnishings. Match up your curtains with a snazzy tablecloth in the same fabric; scatter around a host of bright new cushions; complement your old carpet with a gaily coloured rug; transform an old lamp with an unusual shade – you'll be amazed how all these small touches add up to give your home extra flair and individuality.

By making soft furnishings yourself, all this can be easily achieved within your budget. The shops are full of beautiful fabrics and yarns, and all you have to do is follow the instructions and diagrams to get really professional results. If you have always thought that soft furnishings only involved plain sewing, you'll find lots of delightful ideas for using other techniques – you may be tempted to tackle a gorgeous American patchwork quilt, or learn how to make some super designs in canvas work. For the housewife who enjoys the art of crochet, we show a pattern for an Irish lace bedspread which is an heirloom in itself. By using a wide range of skills such as sewing, embroidery, knitting, crochet, appliqué and canvas work, you can create an endless variety of textures and colours. Also, the patterns in *Soft Furnishings for Your Home* combine the best of both traditional and modern themes, and by using both approaches tastefully, your home will reflect the harmony of an integrated style.

# Contents

# Make a matching tablecloth

Tablecloths no longer create the laundering problems our grandmothers had. With the easy-care fabrics now available you can make non-iron and drip-dry cloths in colours to match your china, to set off a table centre piece, or even to match wallpapers, blinds or curtaining. If the surface of your table needs protection from hot plates, you can buy heat-proof foam material to put underneath the cloth. This is easily cut to the exact size of the table top, and saves hiding a pretty cloth under table mats.

## What you need
☐ Fabric for the tablecloth
☐ Sewing cotton
☐ Trimmings

Measure the top of your table and buy sufficient material to allow for a generous amount to hang down on the four sides. (About 10–14in for an average size rectangular table.) For a plain hem you should allow another 2in all round, but if you are planning a fringe or bobble edging then ½in extra is sufficient.

## How to make a cloth

If the width of the material you are using is not wide enough to be made up into a tablecloth in one piece, make a join using either a plain seam or flat fell seam.

For a plain edge turn up a 1½in hem. Mitre the corners and hand-sew or machine all round for the edges.

For a trimmed edge turn over the fabric ½in on the right side and pin and tack the trimming to cover the raw edge. Sew along the top and the bottom of the trimming to secure it.

If you are using a fairly fine material such as a seersucker or a non-iron fabric, a flat fell seam is more suitable than a plain seam because with this seam all the raw edges are hidden.

## Making seams a feature

If you have to make your cloth out of more than one piece there are several ways of making a special feature out of joining widths of fabric. Usually it looks best if you join the fabric in two seams so that there is a panel running down the centre of the cloth. With a stripe you can cut the central panel so that the stripes run in the opposite direction to the main piece of fabric.

A small floral print can be joined by a plain seam on the right side, the seam edges trimmed to ¼in of the stitching line and the raw edges covered with a braid or ribbon. A plain linen cloth can be made very unusual by applying a central motif using either the zig-zag on your machine, or simple embroidery stitches—for a delicate effect, join strips of linen with knotted insertion stitch.

## To mitre a corner

**1.** Fold over the raw edges ½in and press. Make another fold 1½in from the folded edge and press again firmly. Now open out this fold and turn in the corner on a diagonal line at the point where the two previous pressing lines meet. Press firmly to make a third crease.

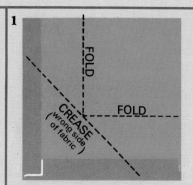

**2.** Trim off the corner to ¼in from the crease, cutting firmly through the turned-in raw edges. Fold at right angles to the trimmed edge right sides together, and sew along the crease line from the point to the folded edge. Turn right side out and gently ease out the point with a knitting needle.

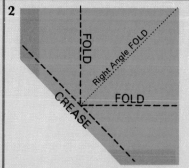

**3.** To a finished mitred corner, turn in the raw edges already pressed over, pin and tack all round the 1½in hem. Machine close to the edge or hand-sew with a neat slip stitch. Press along the edge of a tablecloth on the wrong side, taking care not to iron over the double thickness or it will leave a line on the right side.

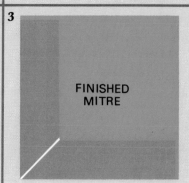

FINISHED MITRE

### Plain seam
With right sides together, machine or back stitch ½in from the edge of the fabric.

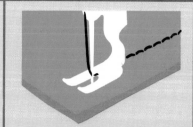

### Neatening seams
To neaten the edges either use the zig-zag on your machine, or turn under the raw edge of the seam allowance and machine close to the edge.

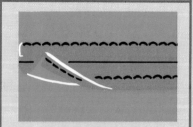

### Flat fell seam
Join as for a plain seam, and trim one side of the seam allowance to within ¼in of the stitching line. Turn over the raw edge of the other side and fold over trimmed edge. Tack and machine near the edge.

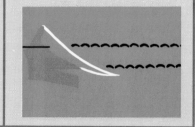

# Round tables - the full treatment

Space saving and charming, round tables look attractive in both traditional and modern decors. This chapter gives instructions for making pretty cloths for them.

## Suitable fabrics

Easily washable dress or furnishing fabrics such as cotton, linen, lawn, man-made fibre mixtures and cotton lace are all suitable for tablecloths. PVC may not hang as well as a softer fabric, but it is spongeable and would be fine for a nursery or kitchen table. Sheeting is also available now in a variety of patterns and colours, and is eminently suitable because of its quality and width.

## Measuring for the cloth

The cloth will cover the table and hang down all round. The depth to which the cloth hangs is a matter of personal choice, but a deep overhang tends to make the cloth look better.

To decide the depth of the overhang, lay a tape measure across the table and let one end drop down until it looks right (figure 1). Multiply the measurement of the overhang by two.

▼ 1. *Measuring for the overhang*

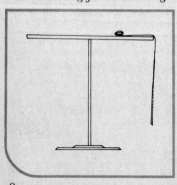

Then measure the diameter of the table, add this measurement to the doubled depth of the overhang and add 1 inch for turnings. An example is given here for a 3ft 6in table with a chosen overhang of 1ft 5in.

| | | |
|---|---|---|
| Overhang (1ft 5in × 2) | = 2ft | 10in |
| Table diameter | = 3ft | 6in |
| Turnings | = | 1in |
| Cloth diameter | = 6ft | 5in |

The final measurement is the most important when buying fabric, but if you draw a little diagram with all the measurements marked on it (figure 2), it will also help you when you make the pattern for the cloth.

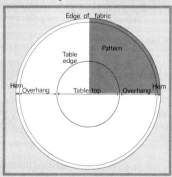

▲ 2. *The vital statistics*

## Fabric widths

A circular tablecloth is made from a square of fabric, each side of the square having the same length as the diameter of the tablecloth.

Furnishing fabrics are usually sold in 48in widths, but it is possible to buy them wider. Dress fabrics, or those which

are most suitable for table-cloths, come in differing widths from 36in to 60in.

Sheeting is very wide indeed and varies in width from 50in to 100in for unbleached (which you can dye), to widths of 70in to 90in for coloured or patterned sheeting. It is, of course, possible to make a round table cloth from a patterned double sheet so long as the diameter of the cloth does not exceed the width of the sheet.

If the width of fabric you choose is less than the diameter of the tablecloth, it will be necessary to join more fabric to the sides of the main piece. It will help you when calculating yardage to remember that the main piece and any extra side pieces must be the same length as the diameter of the tablecloth, and the joined widths must also be equal to the diameter.

## Making the pattern

### You will need

☐ A square of brown wrapping paper, with each side a little longer than the radius (or half the diameter) of the tablecloth

☐ A piece of string, 6 inches longer than the radius of the cloth

☐ A stick of blackboard chalk

☐ A drawing pin

Also, find a large flat surface which will not be spoiled if a pin is pushed into it, such as a wooden kitchen table or lino flooring.

Tie one end of the string round the blackboard chalk and measure the radius of the cloth from the chalk along the length of string. Mark this measurement by pushing the drawing pin through the string.

Lay the square of brown wrapping paper on to the flat surface

could upset the balance of crockery when the table is laid. Figures 4 and 5 show how to cut and join 48in widths to make a cloth with a diameter of 6ft 5in (77in).

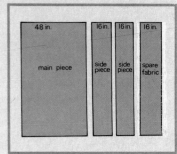

▲ **4.** *How to cut a 48in width*

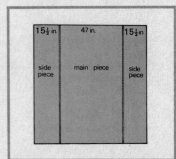

▲ **5.** *Joining the cut pieces*

Join the widths with a flat-fell seam, as shown at the bottom of page 6.
You should now have a square of fabric with each side equal to the diameter of the cloth.

### Cutting out
Fold the prepared square of fabric in half and then in half again, and pin the pattern on to the folded fabric as shown (figure 6).

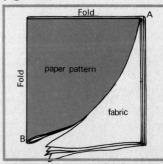

▲ **6.** *Cutting out the fabric*

Cut along the pattern edge. Unpin the pattern and unfold the fabric.

### Making the hem
Snip little 'V's into the edge at 1 inch intervals $\frac{3}{8}$ inch deep (figure 7).

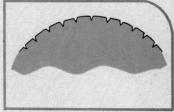

▲ **7.** *Snipping the hem edge*

Turn over the edge $\frac{1}{2}$ inch and pin and tack it down. The 'V's will close up to allow the hem to curve (figure 8).

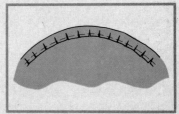

▲ **8.** *Turning over the $\frac{1}{2}$ inch hem*

Pin and tack the bias binding over the turned hem to cover the raw edge.
Stitch on the bias binding (figure 9) neatening the ends by turning them under $\frac{1}{4}$ inch and overlapping them.

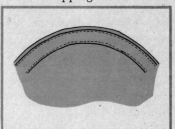

▲ **9.** *Stitching on bias binding*

### Trimming
Machine stitch the trimming you have chosen around the edge of the tablecloth on the right side.

### Good idea
For a round dining table in constant use, protect the tablecloth with a smaller cover made in the same fabric.
Cut a circle of plastic sheeting to the same diameter as that of the table top (this will protect the main cloth from spills), then make a smaller cloth with an overhang of about 6 inches, without trimming, to throw over the top.
This gives an all-over look to the table cover and only the smaller cover need be removed for quick and easy laundering.

and push the drawing pin into the top left hand corner of the paper.
Hold the drawing pin firmly with one hand and draw an arc with the chalk from A, at the top right hand corner of the paper, to B, at the bottom left hand corner (figure 3). Cut along the chalk line. The pattern is a quarter of the area of the cloth, and includes a $\frac{1}{2}$ inch hem allowance.

▼ **3.** *Making the paper pattern*

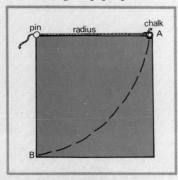

## Making the cloth
### You will need
☐ Fabric for the cloth
☐ Trimming of your own choice. The amount required is the length of the arc A to B multiplied by 4, plus 1 inch for overlapping. Some ideas for trimming are bobble braid, fringing, daisy chains or appliqué motifs
☐ Mercerised cotton to match the fabric
☐ Matching bias binding (the same amount as for the trimming)
☐ Pins
☐ Tacking thread

### Preparing the fabric
If it is necessary to join the fabric, do so now. Join the pieces on to the sides of the main fabric piece; a seam across the middle of the cloth would be very noticeable and

9

# Hardanger table cloth

To make a tea cloth measuring 34 inches square you will need:
- ☐ Cream coloured Hardanger fabric—with 48 threads to 2 inches, 40in by 40in
- ☐ DMC Coton Perlé No.5, 7 skeins dark pink 893; 3 skeins light pink 894
- ☐ DMC 6-cord crochet cotton No. 20, 1 ball 20gr snow-white
- ☐ Pink and cream sewing thread
- ☐ Tapestry needle No. 18

## Planning the design

Use the counted thread guide to plan the outlines of the design. First trace a cross with tacking thread following the grain of the fabric to find the centre (shown opposite on the counted thread guide). Working from the marked centre, trace in running stitches the outlines of the borders and squares using matching thread. The figures on the guide represent the number of ground threads. The extreme outer line indicates the edge of the cloth after the hem has been turned. When planning the cloth, count another 30 threads all round for the hem.

## To strengthen the borders

Strengthen the parts to be openworked by working a row of back stitches inside the motifs with the pink sewing thread, six ground threads from the traced outline. Following the working charts A, B and C, embroider the triangular motifs in satin stitch using DMC Coton Perlé No. 5, so that the points of the triangles touch the traced outlines. Use chart C for the centre border, chart B for outer centre border, chart B for squares and chart A for the outer border. Each square on the charts represents one thread of the fabric. Each thick line represents one straight stitch. Use the light pink thread for the squares and the dark pink thread for the centre and outer borders.

## The openwork squares

To work the openwork squares, cut and draw 4 threads on all four sides immediately below the pink satin stitch triangles. Then leave 8 threads, draw 8 and leave 8 alternately across and down the square. Work the cut openwork using DMC 6-cord crochet cotton following the step-by-step diagrams. Work the inside border in the same way as for the square. For the openwork of the outside border, cut and draw 8 threads along each of the four sides of the tablecloth. Tie groups of 8 threads together with a blanket stitch. In the corners make a cross of threads and tie the centre of the cross with a blanket stitch. Continue the border in the same way on the remaining three sides of the cloth.

## Finishing

When you have completed all the embroidery for the tablecloth you will now need to finish it off by hemming it around all four sides. Finally, press on the wrong side.

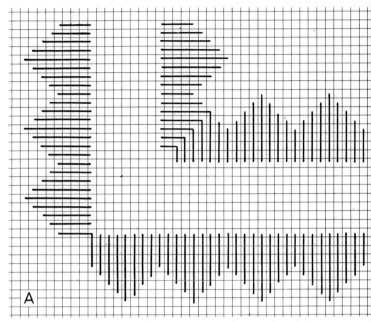

▲ *Chart A for both edges of openwork border on table cloth hem*

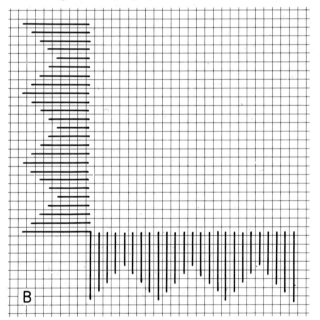

▲ *Chart B for outer edge of central openwork and edges of squares*

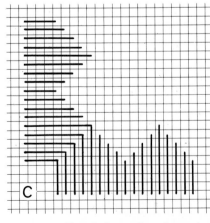

▲ *Chart C for working the inner edge of central openwork*

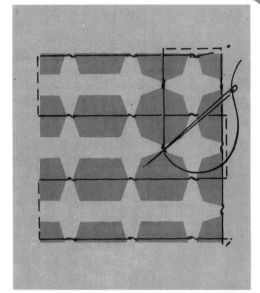

▲ *Openwork stages one and two*

▲ *The openwork squares are edged in light pink, the central and hem areas edged in dark pink*

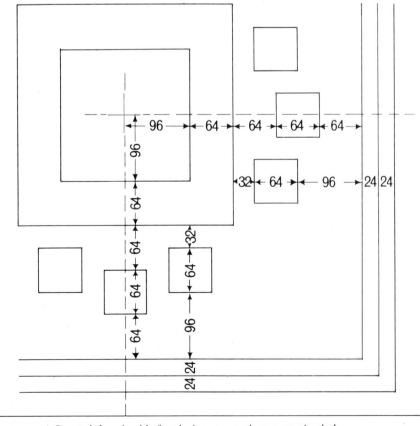

▲ *Counted thread guide for placing openwork areas on the cloth*

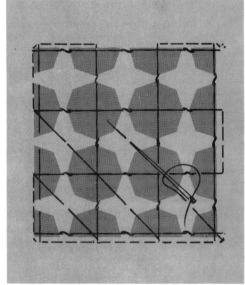

▲ *Openwork stage three*

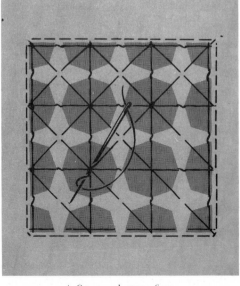

▲ *Openwork stage four*

# Plotting a Sunflower

Plotting the design of a rug from a chart on to the canvas needs care. For complicated designs, such as Oriental patterns, it is easiest to buy a canvas already stencilled with the pattern. If you plot your own pattern, remember that it will show the colour of the stitches in the holes, whereas the actual stitches are worked on the lines of the canvas.

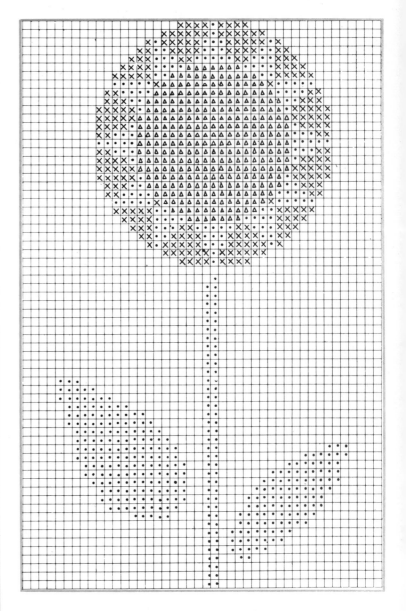

◄ *Use back of rug as colour key to chart — each square represents one knot*

## How to work from a chart

If you are using a chart, it makes it easier if you first mark the design on to the canvas with a felt pen. Draw a vertical line down the centre of the canvas from which to work the pattern. To mark the base of the stalk, count 6 rows up from the bottom of the canvas (after folding over a hem of 1½in), and mark the 2 middle holes, that is, the ones immediately on either side of the centre line. Then, following the chart, count up the holes and mark the design on the canvas. It will simplify later work if the colour changes on the chart are marked with a corresponding felt pen on the canvas.

Once you have grasped the basic idea of the pattern, you can alter it to fit your own canvas. One flower, two leaves and a stalk take 1,018 holes, and 4 units. Work out the total number of holes in the canvas (width holes multiplied by length holes) and subtract from it the number of holes for each flower or flowers. The resulting background number, divided by 320, will give you the number of wool units you need in the background colour. The main thing is to subtract from the total number of holes however many flowers you decide to work on to your canvas.

# The sunflower rug

This sunflower rug is about 24in by 24in and you can use it as a wall picture or backed and filled, as a floor cushion.

Firstly, assemble together all the materials you will be using. You will need:

☐ Canvas 24in wide, 27in long: (24in is a standard width with selvedges, 27in allows an extra 1½in at each end to turn over).

☐ Yarn total 6,400 holes (80 x 80)
    red—1 unit (231 holes)
    yellow—1 unit (294 holes)
    green—2 units (493 holes)
    cream—17 units (5,382 holes)
    ie, each flower with its leaves and stalk
    needs 4 units of wool to cover 1,018 holes

☐ One latchet hook

☐ Extra cream rug wool in a skein, not cut, for binding the edges of the finished rug.

☐ Rug needle

▼ *A finished rug hung on the wall used as a low 'picture' beside a sofa*

▲ *Ideas for rugs using general sunflower motifs*

13

# Shaggy rug story

Rya means shaggy. Because the density of its pile is good insulation against the cold winters the rya is found all over Scandinavia. Originally ryas were woven on a loom with the pile knotted on the warp threads by hand but now you can use a canvas foundation and knot the wool with a latchet hook. The close-up shows the twisted wool, shaggy pile and subtle mingling of colours.

## Colour blended ryas

Rya rugs have an individual style of colouring. Each knot is made of three strands of wool which allows enormous scope for using different shades of colour to build up a rich texture. A colourful rya rug makes an attractive and very cosy addition to your home whether you use it formally on the floor or hung on the wall. A rya floor cushion is quick to make and, as an introduction to the technique, gives a good idea of the versatility of this method of rug making. The cushion can be made any size—24in square makes a comfortable seat and is not too big to move about easily.

### Materials
The canvas to use has 10 squares to 3in and the most suitable wool is a twisted 2 ply coarse rug wool which comes in 25 gramme skeins (4 skeins to a hank). Each skein makes approximately 56 knots.

### Cutting the skeins
After buying the canvas, wool and latchet-hook cut the skeins into pieces the correct length for working. Unravel the skein of wool and holding it fully extended, cut cleanly through the two ends. Then fold these lengths in half and cut again, halve and cut once more. The skein is now divided into eight and you have a pile of cut threads. (It's a good idea to keep the different coloured cut wools in separate polythene bags.) If the cut lengths seem a bit irregular don't bother to trim them as the general look of the rug is shaggy.

### Working a rya
To work the rya, first turn in the rough ends and start to hook in the tufts from left to right (right to left if you are left handed) using three strands of wool in each knot. If you are

making a rug remember to work an edging stitch along one end and partly up both sides before you start. This isn't necessary for a floor cushion as you will be sewing it to a backing, but leave the first and last threads free along the turned in ends.

With skeins of closely related colours rather than complete contrasts you can grade the colours as you wish, increasing or decreasing a colour to get the required intensity or softness. Hook every alternate row, that is, leave one horizontal thread of canvas free between each row of knots.

### Backing a floor cushion
When completed the cushion will need backing with a sturdy upholstery material as this is the side that will be getting the most wear. Choose a colour that blends with the colours you have used for the rya top.

Cut a square of backing material $\frac{3}{4}$in larger than the size of the worked canvas. Put the two right sides together pinning them firmly. Stitch through from the canvas side. On the selvedges stab stitch through to the backing catching each thread of canvas inside the selvedge. Hem the other two edges catching the outside thread of each hole. Leave one side open, turn inside out and stuff the cushion with either two old pillows or a 24in cushion pad, available through most soft furnishing stores.

## 5-movement Latchet-hook method

The method shown below for hooking a rya type rug is the 5 movement method, so-called because to make an individual rya knot, you work in five separate stages. Study the diagrams carefully, follow the instructions, and you will soon become used to the technique.

**1.** To begin, turn up the frayed end of the canvas and insert the latchet hook under the first of the horizontal (weft) threads.

**2.** Hold the two ends of the piece of wool with your left hand and loop it over the hook.

**3.** Pull the hook back through the canvas until the wool loop is halfway through the hole, then push the hook through the loop until the latchet is clear.

**4.** Turn the latchet-hook, place the cut ends in the crook and pull the hook back through the loop. The latchet closes automatically.

**5.** Be sure to pull the knot tight.

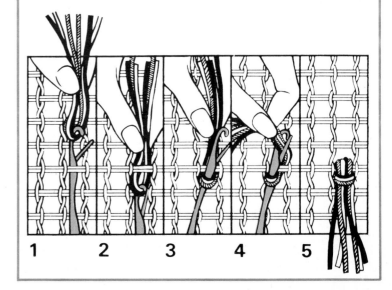

1     2     3     4     5

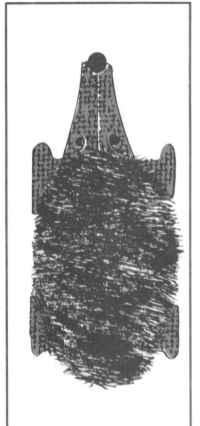

Here's an idea for the nursery—a large, cuddly hedgehog which is soft enough to sit on. Make him from hessian, stuff with kapok or foam, and then work a shaggy rya back. Also shown on this page is a fine example of a real rya rug.

# Rag rugs make a come-back

Bright rag rugs crocheted from strips of material are now enjoying a revival in modern home decor.

## Tearing strips
Rugs are best made from cotton material torn in strips of about ¾ inch wide. Tear the strips lengthwise from the fabric. The longer the piece of fabric the better because the strips will have to be joined less often.

## Joining strips
If you are using leftover lengths of fabric you may be working with strips that are not very long. It saves time finishing ends if both ends are laid along the top of the previous row for a few stitches and worked over using the new strip, so that they are held in place and almost invisible. Any extra length can be trimmed away.

## Alternative material
Rug wool may be used if preferred.

# Rug

## Size
About 46in diameter.

### Tension for this design
2 sts to 1in over tr worked with No. 10·00 hook

## Materials shown here
Strips of cotton ¾in wide in three colours:
A, blue green
B, green
C, yellow

One No.10·00 (ISR) Aero crochet hook

## Working the rug
Using No.10·00 hook and A, work 6ch. Join with ss into first ch to form a circle.

**1st round** 2ch, work 10tr into circles. Join with ss into 2nd of 2ch.

**2nd round** Using B, *1dc between each of next 3tr, 1ch, rep from * to end. Join with ss to first dc.

**3rd round** 2ch, *1dc into next dc, 1ch, rep from * to end. Join with a ss into first of 2ch.

**4th round** Using C, 1ch, work 1dc into each st to end. Join with a ss into first ch.

**5th round** Using A, 3ch, 2tr into next dc, *1tr into next dc, 2tr into next dc, rep from * to end. Join with a ss into 3rd of first 3ch.

**6th round** Using C, 3ch, 1tr into each of next 2tr, *2tr into next tr, 1tr into each of next 3tr, rep from * to end. Join with a ss into 3rd of 3ch.

**7th round** Using B, 1ch, 1dc into each st to end. Join with a ss into first ch.

**8th round** *1dc into next dc, 1tr into next dc, 2tr into next dc, 1tr into next dc, 1dc into next dc, rep from * to end. Join with a ss into first dc.

**9th round** *1dc between 2dc of previous round, 1dc into next st, 2tr between each 3tr on previous round (3 groups of 2tr each), 1dc into next st; rep from * to end. Join with a ss into first dc.

**10th round** Using A, join into centre of point, *3dc into centre st, 7ch, rep from * to end. Join with a ss into first st.

**11th round** 3ch, 6tr into 7ch loop, 1tr into each of 3dc, *7tr into 7ch loop, 1tr into each of next 3dc, rep from * to end. Join with a ss into 3rd of first 3ch.

**12th round** 1ch, work 1dc into each tr. Join with a ss into first ch.

**13th round** Using C, 1ch, work 1dc into each dc. Join with a ss into first ch.

**14th round** 4ch, 1dtr into next dc, 3ch, miss next 2dc, *1dtr into each of next 2dc, 3ch, miss next 2dc, rep from * to end. Join with a ss into 4th of first 4ch.

**15th round** Using C join to first of 3ch with dc, 1dc into each of next 2ch, 1dc between 2dtr, 4dc into ch loop, 1tr between 2dtr, *1dc into each of next 3ch, 1dc between 2dtr, 4dc into ch loop, 1tr between 2dtr, rep from * to end. Join with a ss into first dc.

**16th round** Using A, 1ch, work 1dc into each st. Join with a ss into first ch.

**17th round** 3ch, *work 1tr into each dc. Join with a ss into 3rd of first 3ch.

**18th round** Using B, 1ch, 1dc into each of next 4tr, *2dc into next tr, 1dc into each of next 5dc, rep from * to end. Join with a ss into first dc.

**19th round** 1ch, work 1dc into every st. Join with a ss into first ch.

**20th round** Using C, as 9th.

**21st round** Using B, 3ch, 1tr into next 8dc, *2tr into next dc, 1tr into each of next 9dc, rep from * to end. Join with a ss into 3rd of first 3ch.

**22nd round** 1ch, 1dc into next tr, 2tr into each of next 2tr, 2dtr into each of next 3tr, 2tr into each of next 2tr, 1dc into each of next 2dc, *1dc into each of next 2tr, 2tr into each of next 2tr, 2dtr into each of next 3tr, 2tr into each of next 2tr, 1dc into each of next 2dc, rep from * to end. Join with a ss into first ch. Finish off.

*Rag rug about 46 inches across* ►

16

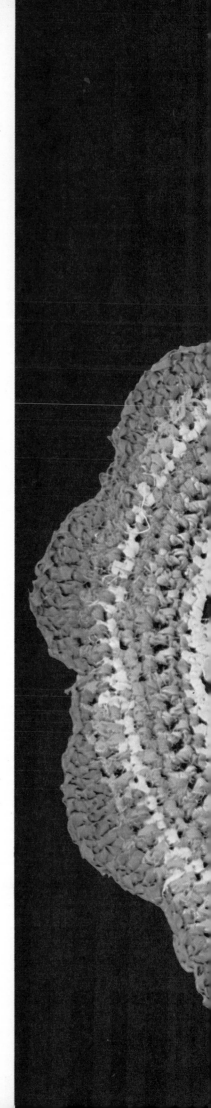

# Collector's cushions

Cushions not only make sinking into chairs and sofas twice as enjoyable but also add decorative shapes and patches of colour to the general scheme of your room.

## It's the filling that counts

What·goes inside a cushion is quite as important as its covering. There are several types of filling—feathers-and-down make the most luxurious but many people now use a Terylene fibre as this is washable. Kapok is cheaper but tends to go lumpy after a while. Foam pads are unwelcoming to lean against and eventually curl at the edges. Many soft furnishing departments now have a large selection of circular and square cushion pads in all sizes with a choice of two qualities of down-and-feathers, all very reasonably priced, which you can cover as you choose.

If you plan to make your own cushion pads you can buy Terylene fibre, kapok or several qualities in feathers-and-down by the pound bag. But, if you are using feathers, remember to make the bag in a down-proof cambric, now available in a selection of colours. For Terylene or kapok fillings a fine fabric such as sateen would be very suitable.

## Simple piped cushion cover

### Materials

For a cushion 18in by 18in.

☐ 37in of a 36in wide material (a bare yard means skimping), or 18½in of a 48in material
   With large-pattern fabrics allow enough extra to position the design centrally on both sides of the cushion.
☐ 2¼yds of No.2 piping cord
☐ 12in zip fastener

*Scatter cushions made from patchwork, crochet and embroidery*

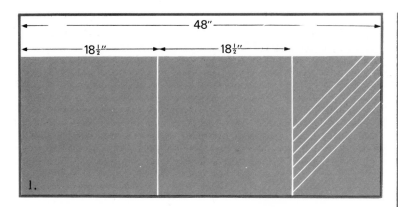

1.

## Making up

To make a cover fit neatly you should make it half an inch smaller all round than the actual cushion size.

Cut out the cushion cover as in the diagram for either 36in (2) or 48in (1) cloth. Join up the bias strips for covering the piping and tack the covered cord around the right side of the cushion top.

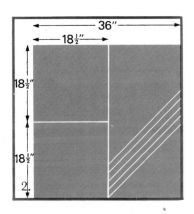

2.

Clip the outside edges of the bias strip at the corners of the cushion and trim away the material so that it lies flat (3). Tack on half of the zip (wrong side uppermost) to the centre of one side of the cushion top. Then using the zipper foot on your sewing machine, stitch all round the cushion top as close to the piping as possible (4).

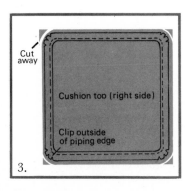

Cut away

Cushion too (right side)

Clip outside of piping edge

3.

Zip (wrong side uppermost)

Top (right side)

4.

Now tack the other half of the zip (again wrong side uppermost) to the back of the cushion, and machine (5). With right sides facing tack the two halves of the cushion together and machine on the previous stitchline for the piping.

Oversew the raw edges and finish off the two ends of the zip. Press cover with a hot iron and turn it right side out. You'll see from the sketch how the piped cushion will look when it is finished (6).

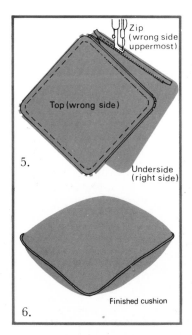

Zip (wrong side uppermost)

Top (wrong side)

5.

Underside (right side)

Finished cushion

6.

*These simple scatter cushions show lots of design ideas for you to copy and from which you may develop ideas of your own. They are all of different shapes and sizes and incorporate techniques such as patchwork, embroidery, appliqué, knitting and fringing. Use cushions to make a hard chair more comfortable, to disguise a bed-sit divan during the day or to brighten dark or plain upholstery. You can also use cushions to unite a colour scheme. For example, use left-overs of curtain material when making your cushions and you will find that the over-all look of the room will hold together far better.*

# Squab cushions

Make a squab or two and add an individual touch to your dining room or kitchen chairs. Full instructions are given in this chapter for making a squab with piped seams and an elastic anchor strip. A method of finishing with tapes and zip is also described plus instructions for buttoning.

## Making the pattern

### You will need
☐ Sheet of newspaper
☐ Sheet of stout brown paper
☐ Scissors to cut the paper
☐ Pencil

A squab should be the same shape as the chair seat which it covers.

Lay the sheet of newspaper across the chair seat and press it down around the front and side edges of the seat. At the back edge of the seat fold the newspaper towards you and make a crease along the back edge of the chair or, if the chair has struts at the back, along the line of struts where they meet the seat. Cut out the newspaper pattern along the creases, shaping it where necessary to fit around the side struts.

Check that the pattern fits the seat exactly. If you need to make sure that the pattern is symmetrical, fold it in half lengthways and see if the cut edges match each other.

When you are satisfied that the newspaper pattern is correct, place it on the brown paper and cut out exactly the same shape. This pattern is without seam allowance.

## The pad

### You will need
☐ A sheet of foam rubber 1 inch thick, slightly larger than the chair seat
☐ A fairly large pair of sharp scissors
☐ A ball-point pen
☐ Masking tape (available from most stationers or do-it-yourself shops)
☐ The brown paper pattern

Lay the pattern onto the sheet of foam rubber and anchor it with small pieces of masking tape. Draw carefully round the pattern with the ball-point pen. Pull off the masking tape, remove the pattern and cut the foam rubber pad out along the pen line.

## The cover

### Suitable fabrics
Squab cushions take a fair amount of wear so it is important to choose a fabric which is firm and will not pull or stretch at the seams. Linen, cotton and repp are all washable while upholstery velvet, corduroy and moquette wear very well but should be dry cleaned.

### You will need
For a squab cushion with piped seams, a slip stitched opening and elastic anchor strip:
☐ Fabric. The amount depends on the size of the chair seat, plus what you will need for covering the piping cord, but as a general rule 1 yard of 36 inch wide fabric will be enough for an average sized cushion
☐ Sewing and tacking thread
☐ A length of piping cord equal to the perimeter of the cushion plus 1 inch
☐ A length of $\frac{1}{2}$ inch wide elastic equal to the width of the cushion at the back
☐ A large press stud
☐ The brown paper pattern

### Making the cover
Fold the fabric, right sides facing, to accommodate the pattern with at least $\frac{1}{2}$ inch of fabric showing all round the pattern.

Pin on the pattern, mark round the edge for the stitching line and then mark a $\frac{1}{2}$ inch seam allowance. Unpin the pattern and cut out the cover.

Cut bias strips $1\frac{1}{2}$ inches wide from the remaining fabric and join them together, as shown in figure 1, to the length of the piping cord.

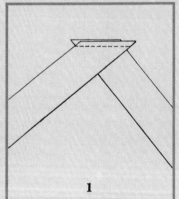

1

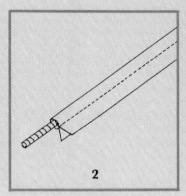

2

Cover the piping cord as shown in figure 2, stitching it with a zipper foot on the sewing machine.

Tack the piping to the right side of one of the cover pieces, as shown in the instructions on page 19 with the stitching line of the piping matching the stitching line on the fabric piece. Stitch the piping in position. Place the other cover piece on to the piped piece, right sides facing, and stitch them together along the stitching line for the piping. Stitch along three sides only, leaving the back edge open. Turn the cover right side out.

Insert the foam rubber pad into the cover and close the opening with slip stitch.

To secure the squab to the chair, sew the socket half of the press stud to the left hand back corner on the underside

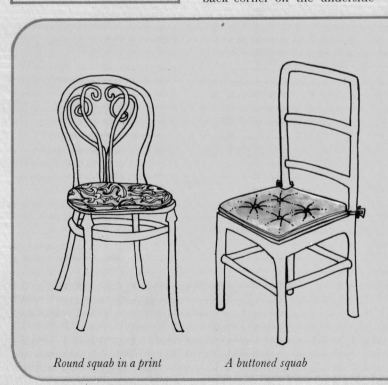

Round squab in a print          A buttoned squab

of the squab, and the elastic to the right hand back corner. Neaten the free end of the elastic and sew the ball half of the press stud to the neatened end (figure 3).

Place the squab in position on the chair, pass the elastic under the chair seat and close the press stud.

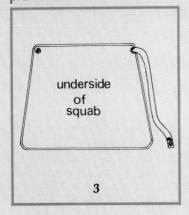

3

## Tapes and zip finish

### You will need
- [ ] The brown paper pattern
- [ ] Foam rubber pad
- [ ] Cover fabric
- [ ] Piping cord
- [ ] Sewing and tacking thread
- [ ] 1 yard $\frac{1}{2}$ inch wide straight tape (in a matching colour)
- [ ] A zip, 2 inches less in length than the width of the back edge of the squab

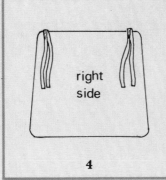

4

Fold the fabric, cut and mark the cover pieces and cover the piping cord as before.

Cut the straight tape into two 18 inch lengths and fold each of these in half. Place the tapes on the right side of one of the cover pieces as shown in figure 4, and pin.

Tack on the piping cord so that the tapes are sandwiched between the piping and the

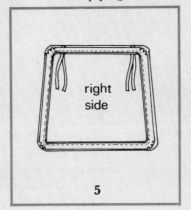

5

cover (figure 5). Insert one half of the zip as instructed on page 19, and then stitch piping, tapes and zip in one operation.

Tack and stitch the other half of the zip in position, join the cover pieces and turn the cover right side out.

### Using matching ties
Instead of straight tape it is a pretty idea to use matching ties made of the cover fabric. Cut a long strip from the cover fabric 2 inches wide and 36 inches long, fold this in half lengthways, right sides facing, and stitch along the length. Turn the strip of fabric right side out, cut it in half so that you have two 18 inch lengths and neaten all the ends. Stitch the strips to the cover as shown in the instructions for the straight tapes.

## Buttoned squabs

### You will need
- [ ] 5 $\frac{3}{4}$in button moulds
- [ ] 5 $\frac{1}{2}$in shirt buttons
- [ ] Scraps of the cover fabric for covering the button moulds
- [ ] Button and tacking thread

Decide where you wish the buttons to be placed and mark

these points with tacking thread on each side of the squab.

Cover the button moulds with fabric. Place each covered button in the correct position on the upper side of the squab and a small button on the underside directly beneath the top button. Sew the covered button to the small button

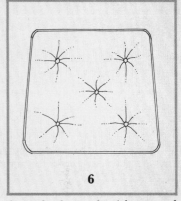

6

through the pad with several firm stitches, pulling the thread taut as you sew. Fasten off securely on the underside of the squab (figure 6).

### Handy hint
To remove the cover for washing or cleaning simply snip the threads below the small buttons and remove all the buttons. The cover will then slip off easily and it is a simple matter to sew on the buttons again when the cover is replaced.

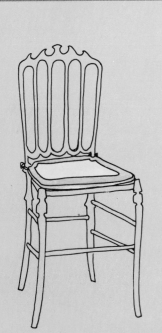
*Squab in contrasting colours*

*Squab in a simple check*

*Squab with bold appliqué*

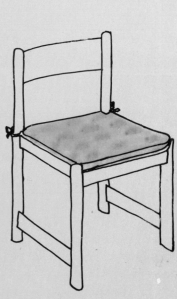
*Plain squab in a bold colour*

# Patching passions

Patchwork is both interesting and rewarding because of the infinite number of ways the various shapes can be combined. This chapter shows some simple yet attractive patterns you can build up with the more familiar shapes.

Before beginning the work, cut out paper patterns from the templates, juggle them around to form various designs, and choose the final overall combination you like best.

If you are new to patchwork, it is wiser to start with the square, hexagon, long hexagon and octagon shapes, as it is easier to tack the material over wider angles. The sharp points of diamonds can be very tricky, especially if you are working in a heavy fabric.

Here are a few ideas for building up patchwork designs using different combinations of shapes. For small projects like cushions or tea cosies a simple design is more effective. On a large article such as a bedcover there is ample space to work out a more ambitious and complex pattern.

*The basic patchwork shapes* ▼ *and some ideas for attractive patterns* ►

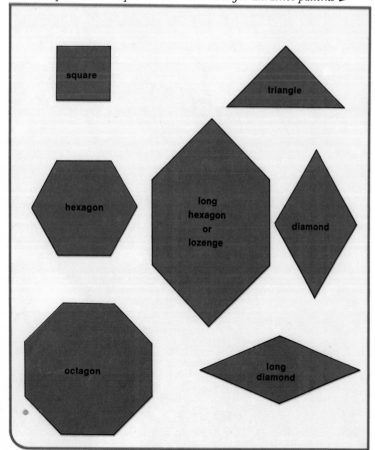

square

triangle

hexagon

long hexagon or lozenge

diamond

octagon

long diamond

## Pattern names

Patchwork patterns, like recipes, have travelled from country to country acquiring local amendments and new names. America, a great country for patchwork since the first English and Dutch settlers took the craft there, has such fascinating old names as Slave chain and Indian trail. Many patchwork names are descriptive — Ocean wave is lines of hexagons rising and falling in a zigzag, Windmill is triangles joined at a point, Dog's tooth a row of sharp triangles, and a pattern made of big and small stars is called Milky Way. Of single shapes, an equilateral hexagon is called a Honeycomb, a long hexagon a Church window, and coffin-shaped hexagon a Coffin. The liberal use of hexagons is characteristic of English work.

## Patchwork for cushions

These two cushion designs use the wider-angled templates.

### Top cushion

The design has been carefully planned, using the border pattern in the fabric for the patches, to enhance the design on the cushion. This is where a perspex template or a 'window' gives you an advantage. The five eight-pointed star shapes are the ground material, where the patchwork has left an interesting shape in the middle. To fit this design on to a cushion 17in square, use $\frac{3}{4}$in octagon and square templates.

### Bottom cushion

This is 17 inches square and has a design using $1\frac{1}{4}$in lozenge shapes. The interest is in the contrast between plain and patterned fabrics, as only one template shape was used.

### How to make up

Join together the different patches to make up the design, tack round the outside edges and appliqué the patchwork to the ground material.

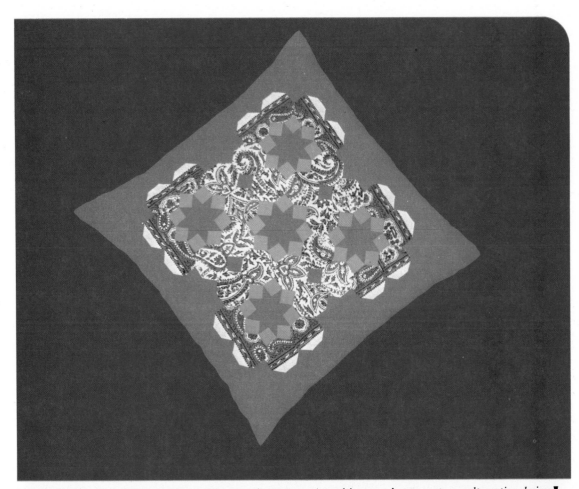

*Octagonal and square patches make up this attractive pattern* ▲ *and lozenge shapes create an alternative design* ▼

# Cushion shapes

These cheerful cushions will brighten any room and are simple enough to make in an evening. There's no need to worry about the problem of keeping them fresh and bright—the covers are detachable and can be taken off and cleaned whenever disaster strikes. Trace patterns are overleaf.

## Your shopping list

**Fish cushion**
- ☐ ¾yd 36in wide orange hessian
- ☐ ¾yd 36in wide unbleached calico for lining
- ☐ Four 9 inch squares of felt, in pink, red, orange and crimson
- ☐ Mercerised cotton thread in orange
- ☐ 1 lb bag of kapok*
- ☐ 12 inches of bias binding in orange
- ☐ 3 press studs
- ☐ Tube of rubber solution glue
- ☐ Tracing paper

**Bird cushion**
- ☐ ¾yd 36in wide purple hessian
- ☐ ¾yd 36in wide unbleached calico for lining
- ☐ Four 9 inch squares of felt in mauve, pink, purple and blue
- ☐ Mercerised cotton thread in purple
- ☐ 12 inches of bias binding in purple
- ☐ 3 press studs
- ☐ Tube of rubber solution glue
- ☐ Tracing paper

\* The 1 lb bag of kapok is sufficient to stuff both cushions

## The fish cushion

**The pattern** Trace the shape of the fish, with its scales, eye and mouth, on to a sheet of plain tracing paper. Cut the traced pattern out along the outlines.

**Cutting the fabric** Fold the hessian in half, right sides together. If it is difficult to decide which is the right side, make a small pencil mark on one side of the fabric and think of that side as the right side.
Pin the pattern on to the folded hessian making sure that there is at least ½ inch of fabric showing all the way round.
With a soft pencil draw round the outline of the fish at the edge of the pattern and again ½ inch away from the edge. Unpin the pattern. The outside line is the cutting line and the inside line is the sewing line. Cut out the fish shape.
Pin the fish pattern on to the folded calico and mark and cut in the same way for lining.

**Marking the decorations** Repin the pattern to the right side of one of the hessian fish shapes and mark with tacking, through the pattern, the lines of the scales, and the position of the eye and mouth. Pull the pattern away gently (if it tears too much trace another pattern) and mark the right side of the other hessian piece in the same way.

**Cutting the decorations** Trace separate patterns for the eyes and the mouth and using these patterns cut out the eye and mouth shapes in felt. You will need 2 outer eyes, 2 inner eyes and 2 mouths.

For each hessian piece cut out 34 little triangles, with 1¼ inch sides, in 4 different colours, 8 pink, 8 orange, 9 red and 9 crimson. These are the scales.

**Making up the calico lining** Pin and tack the calico fish shapes together, right sides facing. Machine stitch round the edge on the stitching line leaving a 3 inch opening near the tail (figure 1). Turn right sides out and stuff with kapok until it is firm but not bulky. Sew up the opening.

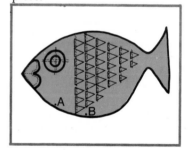

▲ **1.** *Stitch the calico lining shape*

**Making up the hessian cover** Using the photograph as a colour guide, glue the decorations lightly on to the right side of one of the hessian pieces where indicated by the tacked markings. Then machine stitch the decorations down with two parallel lines of stitching. Two lines of stitching make an extra strong finish.
Repeat with the other hessian piece.

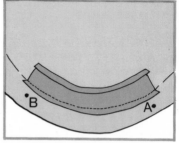

▲ **2.** *Mark openings on hessian pieces*

Mark the openings A and B with a pencil (figure 2). Cut 2 pieces of bias binding each 6 inches long. Open out the edge of one of the bias strips and with right sides facing pin and tack it to one of the hessian pieces between A and B (figure 3). Stitch, fold the binding over and stitch the other folded edge down (figure 4). Repeat for the other hessian piece.

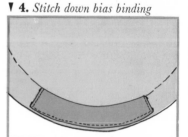

▲ **3.** *Tack bias binding along opening*
▼ **4.** *Stitch down bias binding*

Pin and tack the hessian pieces right sides facing and machine stitch round the edge on the stitching line. Leave the opening between A and B but make sure that the stitching is very firmly finished off (figure 5). Turn the cover right sides out and press carefully.

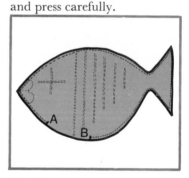

▲ **5.** *Stitch hessian pieces together*

**Finishing off** Sew the 3 press studs on to the bias binding. Insert the stuffed calico lining and close the press studs.

## The bird cushion

Make the pattern, mark and cut out the hessian and calico bird shapes as for the fish cushion. Mark the positions for the feathers and eyes, then stitch and stuff the calico lining as before.

**Cutting out the decorations** Make patterns for the beak and the eyes then using these patterns cut out the beak and eye shapes in felt. You will need 2 beak shapes, 2 inner eye shapes and 2 outer eye shapes.

▲ *Fish and bird shapes make cheerful cushions for any room and are simple to sew*

For each hessian piece cut out 29 little circles about an inch in diameter, (you can use a suitably sized coin), in four different colours; 6 mauve, 6 pink, 9 purple and 8 blue. These are the feathers.

**Making up** Using the illustration as a colour guide, glue the eyes and feathers on to the right side of each hessian bird

shape. Stitch, using two parallel lines of stitching as in the fish cushion. Mark and neaten the openings as before.

Stitch the beak pieces together along 2 sides, turn the beak inside out and stuff with a little kapok.

Place the two hessian bird shapes right sides facing with the beak sandwiched between

them pointing inwards (figure 6).

Pin, tack and stitch the hessian pieces together, leaving an opening between A and B. Turn right sides out and press. Do not press the beak.

Finish off as for the fish cushion.

**6.** *Stitch beak between hessian* ▶

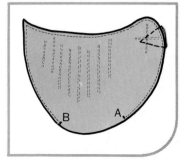

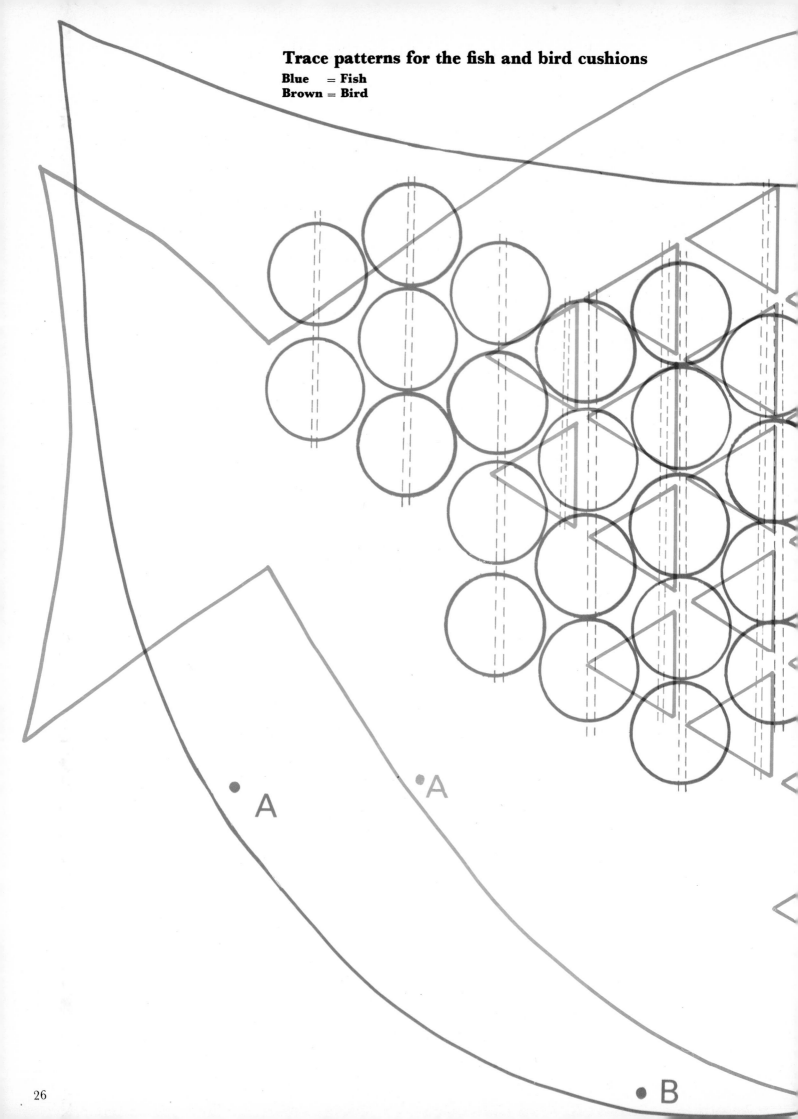

**Trace patterns for the fish and bird cushions**
Blue    = Fish
Brown = Bird

A

A

B

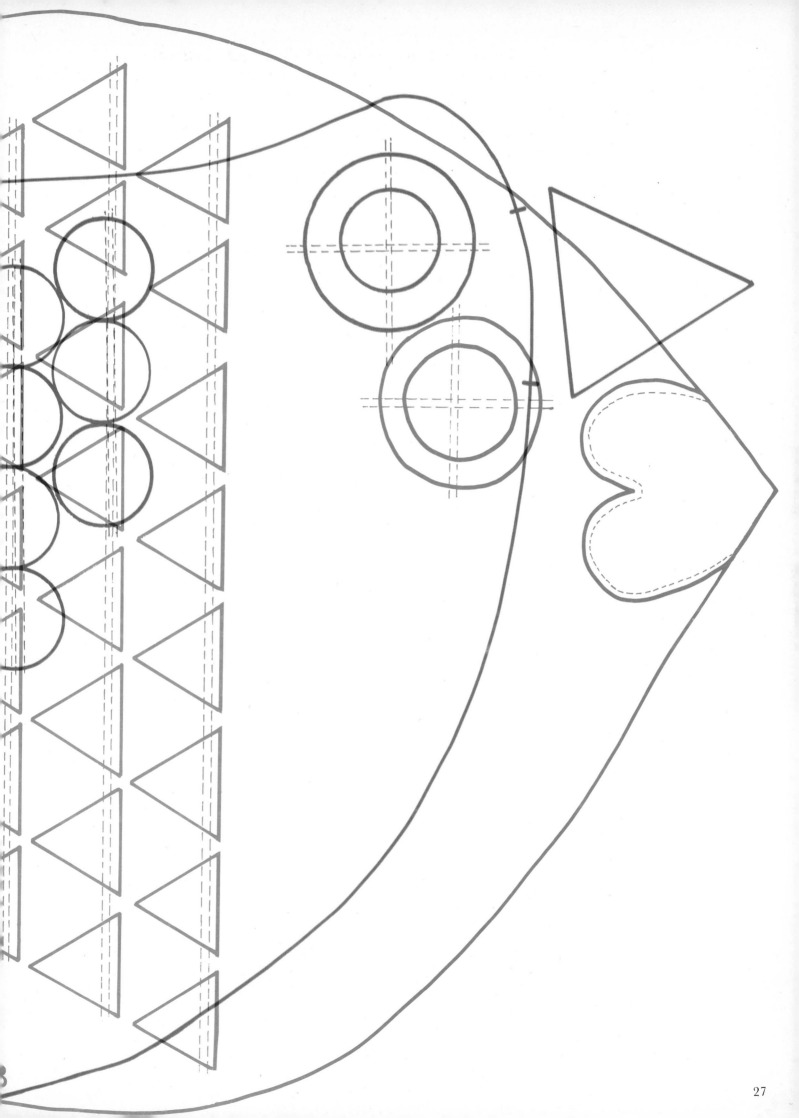

# A nosegay of summer daisies

Flowers embroidered on gingham give a refreshing new look to furnishings, the softness of the design contrasting with the fabric background. Make this gay daisy-embroidered cushion to brighten a bedroom, to add a splash of colour to a kitchen or sun room, or for a set of garden chairs.

## Materials you will need
- ☐ ½yd 36in wide gingham
- ☐ Cushion pad 14in by 14in (finished cushion 13in by 13in)
- ☐ 10in zip
- ☐ Crewel needle size 7
- ☐ Stranded cotton, 1 skein each dark yellow and bright green; 2 skeins each lemon yellow and brown, 6 skeins white

## Stitches and yarns
The stitches used in this design are stem stitch, chain stitch, long and short stitch, French knots and Roumanian stitch. The entire design is worked in stranded cotton using a varying number of strands for the different parts.

## Transferring the design
First cut the fabric down the centre fold and mark the centre of one piece with lines of tacking. The best way to transfer the design on to the fabric is to first make a tracing, positioning it centrally.

## Working the design
**Flowers.** The petals on the flowers are embroidered in long and short stitch using three strands of cotton. The outlines of the petals are worked in stem stitch with two strands. Some of the petals on each flower can be stitched using five strands of cotton to give a raised look.
**Buds.** Some of the buds are embroidered with brown and the rest with bright green, using four strands of cotton. The edges of the buds are in stem stitch and filled with long and short stitch.
**Bud petals.** The petals on the buds are worked with two chain stitches, a small one inside a larger one, using four strands of cotton.
**Stems.** Work the stems in stem stitch, using brown and bright green alternately, using four strands of cotton. The stems are caught together with three Roumanian stitches in yellow.
**Centres.** The centres of the daisies are first worked in stem stitch, working the outer edge of the circle first and working in to the centre. Then several French knots are made over the stem stitch.

## To make up
When all the embroidery is complete, press carefully on the wrong side and trim the fabric to the size of the cushion, plus ⅝ inch seam allowances all round. Make up the cushion according to the instructions on the bottom of page 39, leaving a 10 inch opening for inserting the zip.

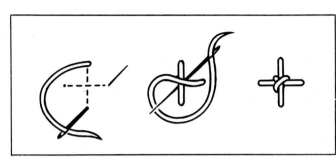

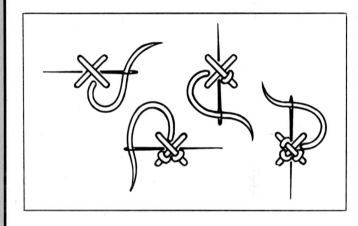

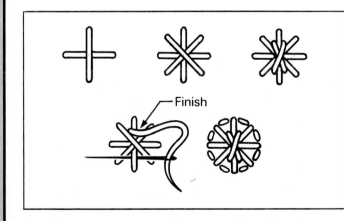

Finish

# Razzamatazz cushions in chevron crochet

Here is a fresh and charming furnishing idea for using up oddments of yarn. It is also an opportunity for you to practise increasing and decreasing in simple double crochet to shape fabric in an exciting way.

### Size
Approximately 14½in across the width of the cushion

### Materials shown here
Pingouin Classique Crylor
One 50grm ball each of main shade, A, and contrast colours, B, C and D
One No.4·00 (ISR) crochet hook
One round cushion pad 14in wide or foam filling and lining to make a cushion insert to these dimensions

## Cushion

Using No.4·00 (ISR) hook and A, make 214ch.
**Base row** Into 2nd ch from hook work 1dc, 1dc into each of next 9ch, *into next ch work 3dc, 1dc into each of next 10ch, insert hook into next ch and draw yarn through, miss 1ch, insert hook into next ch and draw yarn through, yrh and draw through all loops on hook, 1dc into each of next 10ch, rep from * to last 11ch, work 3dc into next ch, 1dc into

*Multi-colour scheme from odds and ends of yarn for a gay effect* ►
*A modern look with four colours and a pompon trim* ▼

32

each of next 10ch. Turn.

**1st patt row** 1ch, dec one st by inserting hook into back loop only of next dc and drawing yarn through, insert hook into back loop only of next dc and draw yarn through, yrh and draw through all loops on hook, work 1dc into each of next 9dc working into back loop only of each dc, *3dc into next dc, (which is the centre dc of the inc dc in previous row), working into back loop only, 1dc into each of next 10dc working into back loop only, dec in next 3dc by inserting hook into back loop only of next dc and drawing yarn through, miss 1dc, insert hook into back loop only of next dc and draw yarn through, yrh and draw through all loops on hook, 1dc into each of next 10dc working into back loop only, rep from * to end of row, dec one st in last 2dc by inserting hook into back loop only of last dc but one and drawing yarn through, insert hook into back loop only of next dc and draw yarn through, yrh and draw through all loops on hook. Turn.

This row forms patt and is rep throughout.

Keeping patt correct work 6 rows in all in A, 6 rows B, 2 rows C, then 4 rows each in D, A, C, B, D, A and C. Fasten off leaving an end long enough to join seam. Darn in all ends.

## To make up

DO NOT PRESS.
Join side seams to form a circle taking care to match stripes.
Join the sides of each chevron point at one end tog and catch the point of each chevron and fasten off securely. Insert cushion pad and complete chevron points at other end in same way.
Trim one side of the cushion with a large crochet covered button, for which you use colour A for contrast and the other side with a pompom using A, B, C and D.

▲ *When the crochet is completed it makes a strip. The sides of each point are seamed and the strip joined to form a circle. The points are gathered at top and bottom to meet*
▼ *Cushion with button trim*

# Looped, striped and lacy cushions

Three rich-looking knitted cushion patterns and an opportunity for you to practise your knitting techniques.

## Looped effects

The looped cushion can also be given a different appearance by working several rows of one colour then changing to a contrast of a different tone of the first colour. For example, gradual shading towards the centre would give a flower-like appearance.

## Garter stitch

The garter stitch square can be used in various different ways to give a variety of effects both in the arrangements of the squares and in the mixing of self coloured squares with striped squares. Colour effects can also give different appearances to the same arrangement of squares.

## Lace effects

You may wish to try different lace effects from your own repertoire for suitable stitches. or experiment with the colour of the cushion slip beneath the lace pattern. A strong contrast will emphasise the lace effect.

## Mohair loop cushion

### Size

Approx 17in diameter, adjustable as required

> **Tension for this design**
> 4 sts and 7 rows to 1in over garter st worked on No.6 needles

### Materials shown here

Wendy Pompadour
10 balls
One pair No.6 needles
One cushion pad

### Base

Begin at centre.
Cast on 9 sts.
**1st and alt rows** K.
**2nd row** Inc in each st to last st, K1.
**4th row** *K1, inc, rep from * to last st, K1.
**6th row** *K2, inc, rep from * to last st, K1.
**8th row** *K3, inc, rep from * to last st, K1.
**10th row** *K4, inc, rep from * to last st, K1.
Continue inc in this way until work measures 8½in from cast on edge. Cast off.

### Top

Begin at centre.
Cast on 9 sts.
**1st row** K1, * insert needle as if to K and wind yarn over needle point and 2 fingers twice then round needle point and draw loops through, return to left hand needle and K tog tbl loops and original st—called ML—, K1, rep from * to end.
**2nd row** Inc in each st to last st, K1.
**3rd and every alt row** K1, *ML, K1, rep from * to end.
**4th row** *K1, inc, rep from * to last st, K1.
**6th row** *K2, inc, rep from * to last st, K1.
**8th row** *K3, inc, rep from * to last st, K1.
Continue inc in this way on every alt row 8 times, working loop row on odd rows. Work until the same size as base.

### To make up

Seam edges leaving an opening for cushion pad. Insert pad and close opening.

## Garter stitch cushion

### Size

16in square

> **Basic yarn tension**
> 5½ sts and 7½ rows to 1in over st st worked on No.8 needles

### Materials shown here

Patons Double Knitting wool
9 balls main shade, A, white
1 ball contrast colour, B, tan
1 ball contrast colour, C, red
1 ball contrast colour, D, black
One pair No.8 needles
16in cushion pad

### Front

Using No.8 needles and A, cast on 3 sts.
**1st row** K.
**2nd row** Inc by K twice into same st, inc, K1.
**3rd row** K.
**4th row** Inc, K2, inc, K1.
**5th row** K.
Continue inc in this way inside the edge sts on next and every alt row until there are 31 sts.
Break off A.
Keeping inc correct as before, work 12 rows B, 12 rows C, 12 rows D. Break off D and complete with A. 67 sts.
K1 row.
Dec one st at each side inside edge sts, on next and every alt row until 3 sts rem.
K 1 row. Cast off.
Work 3 more squares in the same way. Join squares together, matching stripes carefully.

### Back

Work as given for Front, using A only for each square.

### To make up

Seam Back and Front together, leaving one side open. Insert cushion pad and slip stitch remaining side tog.

## Lacy cushion

### Size

12in by 17in

> **Basic yarn tension**
> 6 sts and 8 rows to 1in over st st worked on No.9 needles

### Materials shown here

Wendy Courtellon Double Knitting
8 balls
One pair No.7 needles
12in by 17in cushion pad

### Note

To work Tw2F and Tw2B, see Knitting Know-how, chapter 16

### Front

Using No.7 needles cast on 67 sts.
K5 rows.
Commence patt.
**1st row** K1, *Tw2F, K4, yfwd, sl 1, K1, psso, K3, Tw2B, rep from * to last st, K1.
**2nd and every alt row** K1, P to last st, K1.
**3rd row** K1, *Tw2F, K2, K2 tog, yfwd, K1, yfwd, sl 1, K1, psso, K2, Tw2B, rep from * to last st, K1.
**5th row** K1, *Tw2F, K1, K2 tog, yfwd, K3, yfwd, sl 1, K1, psso, K1, Tw2B, rep from * to last st, K1.
**7th row** K1, *Tw2F, K2 tog, yfwd, K5, yfwd, sl 1, K1, psso, Tw2B, rep from * to last st, K1.
**8th row** As 2nd.
Rep these 8 rows 11 times more. K5 rows. Cast off.

### Back

Work as given for Front.

### To make up

Join seams on 3 sides. Insert cushion pad and slip stitch remaining side together.
If required make 4 large tassels and attach one to each corner.

*The garter stitch cushion square with its three-colour diagonal band can be grouped in a variety of ways* ►

34

# Garden cushions in wool embroidery

Brighten up your garden furniture with these brilliantly coloured cushions. Embroider some and leave others plain. Using chunky tappiserie wool, the design is worked in simple stitches such as chain stitch, stem stitch and fly stitch. Use the stitches and colours suggested or experiment with your own choice. The same design could look interesting translated into appliqué.

To make a cushion measuring 17 inches in diameter you will need:
- [ ] ½yd 54in furnishing fabric
- [ ] 2¾yds contrast colour piping
- [ ] Sewing cotton to match fabric
- [ ] Cushion pad 18 inches in diameter, 2½ inches deep
- [ ] Large tapestry needle
- [ ] 2 button moulds 1 inch in diameter (plain cushion only)

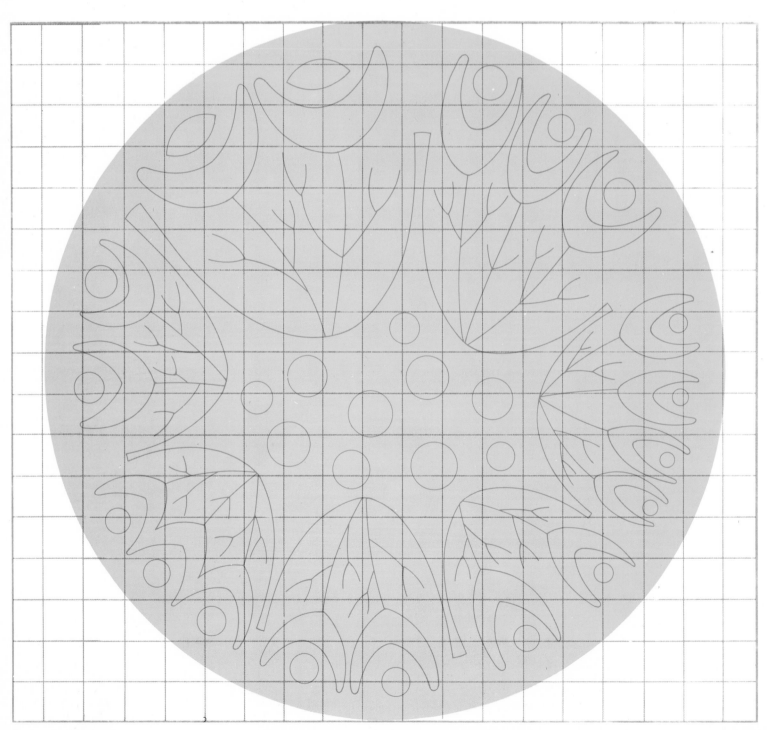

☐ DMC Laine à Broder
Tapisseries No.13 in the
following colours:
1 skein each of burgundy
red 7110; wine red 7108;
scarlet 7606 and yellow
7431

## To transfer pattern and design

Draw the pattern and design
from the chart onto 1 inch
squared paper. Trace the
pattern and design onto tracing
paper and cut out. Lay the
pattern onto the folded fabric
and cut out two circles for the
top and bottom of the cushion,
allowing $\frac{5}{8}$ inch turnings all
round the edge. Cut a strip
for the gusset measuring $49\frac{1}{4}$
inches long and $3\frac{3}{4}$ inches deep.
Take one circle of the fabric
and trace the outline only onto
this. Now take the second circle
of fabric and trace the outline
and design onto the right side
of the fabric, using carbon
paper or small running stitches
through the tracing paper and
the fabric.

## The stitches used

The central area of the design
is worked in outlines of French
knots in yellow. The stalks
are in chain stitch, stem stitch
and fly stitches using scarlet
and wine red. The stylised
flower heads are worked in
satin stitch in wine red and
burgundy red.

## To make up cushion

Pin and tack the piping round
the outline of the cushion top
and bottom. Pin the gusset to
the top, easing it round the
circle until both ends meet.
Pin, tack and stitch the gusset
seam. Tack the gusset to the
top and stitch as close to the
piping as possible. If stitching
by machine use a piping foot.
For a smooth finish, cut notches
on seam allowance all round.
Stitch bottom of cushion in
the same way but leave about
10 inches open to insert cushion
pad. Turn cover to the right
side and insert pad. Stitch the
10 inch opening by hand.

◄ *The design to trace and enlarge*

*Bright cushions for sunny days* ►

# Gay cushions in appliqué

Felt is the easiest material for beginners to try appliqué. There is no problem of matching fabric weights and textures or of having to cope with fraying edges, which would mean finishing off the shapes before applying. With felt, simply cut and stitch. Felt is stocked by most fabric departments and is available in 9 inch or 12 inch squares, or by the yard in varying widths, in a wide range of colours. These brilliant felt cushions show ways of using cut and stitch appliqué.

## Felt appliqué cushions

The two cushions shown in the photograph cleverly combine both the cut and stitch and the cut-out methods.

**Materials you will need:**
- ☐ Four pieces of felt 20in by 20in, two orange and two yellow
- ☐ One piece of felt 20in by 20in in pink
- ☐ One piece of felt 12in by 12in in mauve
- ☐ Two pieces of paper 20in by 20in for making paper patterns (newspaper will do)
- ☐ Two cushion pads 20in by 20in or kapok for stuffing
  **NB.** Felt should be dry cleaned but do remember, if you use kapok—which is cheaper than cushion pads—the cushions cannot be dry cleaned unless kapok is removed
- ☐ Two 12in zippers, one orange and one yellow (if you are using cushion pads)
- ☐ Matching sewing threads, or colourless nylon thread which can be used for both cushions.

## How to cut out paper patterns

**1.** Fold each of the paper squares in half, then quarter, and then diagonally in a triangle.

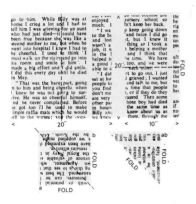

**2.** On one of the folded triangles, draw cutting lines as indicated in the diagram. Cut evenly along these lines through all layers. Put aside the cut-out pieces (4 of each pattern) and pin the large pattern cut-out on to one piece of orange felt.

**3.** On the second folded paper triangle, draw cutting lines as indicated in the diagram. Cut out and keep only the cut-out pieces (eight of one pattern and one centre pattern), discarding the remainder of the paper square.

**4.** Carefully unfold all paper patterns and label them A—D as shown.

### Cutting out the felt

**5.** Pin patterns to appropriate colours of felt, arranging them very carefully to follow the diagrams. As patterns A (mauve) and B (pink) will be used to fill in the cut-outs of the orange cushion, leave $\frac{1}{4}$in seam allowance on these patterns. Cut all other patterns to the exact size.

Tack the pattern on to the felt and remove the pins. Use a small pair of scissors with very sharp points to begin cutting out each shape, then continue with normal cutting-out scissors. If the raw edges are not smooth, trim with the small scissors. When cutting out is completed, you will have four mauve A with $\frac{1}{4}$in seam allowance, four pink B with $\frac{1}{4}$in seam allowance, four orange A, four orange B, one pink C, and eight pink D shapes. The orange felt will also have four A cut-outs and four B cut-outs.

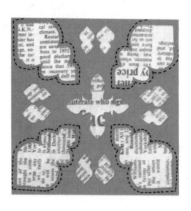

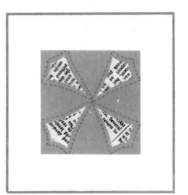

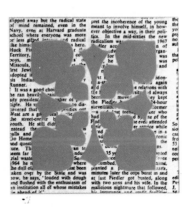

### To make the orange cushion

**6.** Pin and tack four mauve A shapes and four pink B shapes to the wrong side of the orange felt, filling in the eight cut-outs. Machine, with a straight stitch, on the right side of the felt, as close to the raw edge as possible. (If you want a more decorative finish, use a zigzag stitch.) Next, still working on the right side, pin, tack and machine in place four pink D shapes.

Remove all tacking threads.

### To make the yellow cushion

**7.** Criss-cross the yellow felt square with tacking thread as shown in the diagram, which will enable you to position the shapes correctly. Pin, tack and machine the remaining four orange A shapes and four orange B shapes on to the right side of the yellow felt. Then pin, tack and machine the one pink C and the remaining four pink D shapes into position as shown.

Remove all tacking threads.

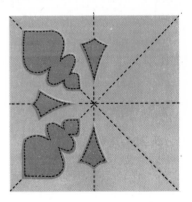

### To make up cushions

**8.** Place plain orange and yellow felt pieces to appliquéd pieces with right sides facing. Tack and machine around the sides with $\frac{1}{4}$in seam allowance, leaving a 12in opening along one side for inserting the zippers. Turn to the right side. Pin and tack, then stitch zippers into place. Insert cushion pads.

If you are stuffing with kapok, tease it out first, then do not pack tight but fill gently.

Turn in seam allowance and stitch up the openings securely by hand.

# Cushioned with an apple

This succulent apple in vibrant colours shows an interesting use of chain stitch for a bold effect.

To make the cushion 16 inches by 16 inches you will need:

- ☐ ½yd 36 inch wide even weave linen
- ☐ Cushion pad 1 inch larger than finished size of cushion
- ☐ Reel of mercerised sewing cotton to match background fabric
- ☐ Clarks Anchor Stranded Cotton in the following colours: One skein orange 0316; one skein dark green 0246; two skeins green 0268
- ☐ Anchor Soft Embroidery Cotton in the following colours: Four skeins red 0335; two skeins pink 025
- ☐ 12 inch zip
- ☐ Tracing paper
- ☐ Graph paper

## To enlarge the design

Trace and enlarge the design to measure 11 inches from the tip of the top leaf to the lower edge of the apple. Trace the enlarged design onto tracing paper.

▼ *Trace and enlarge this design to the required size*

## Transferring the design

Fold the fabric and cut the piece in two. Mark the centre with rows of tacking stitches each way. Work a line of tacking stitches 2 inches in from the outer edges to form a square measuring 16 inches by 16 inches, to mark the outer edges of the cushion. Pin the traced design in position $2\frac{3}{4}$ inches up from the lower line of tacking stitches and centralising the design between the two vertical lines. Using the matching sewing cotton transfer the design to the background fabric stitching all the lines of design through the tracing paper. When all the lines have been marked with tacking the paper is torn away. If the tacking stitches are well covered with embroidery they need not be removed when the design is completed.

## Stitches

Begin with the orange shape. Use six strands of cotton, and start the chain stitching from the outer edge of each shape, working towards the centre. This ensures a well defined outline. Work the deep pink area next and finally the red. Leave gaps in the chain stitch filling where indicated on the design and fill these with bullion knots. The bullion knots are also worked with six strands of cotton and with three twists round the needle. Work the apple leaves in stem stitch filling with the veins in stem stitch, using four strands of cotton. The calyx at the bottom of the apple is formed by working three detached chain stitches one inside the other starting with the outer. The stalk is worked in four separate rows of stem stitch using four strands of cotton.

## To make up the cushion

When the embroidery is completed, press the work lightly over a damp cloth and a thick, soft pad to avoid flattening the bullion knots.

Make up the cushion according to the instructions given at the bottom of the previous page and insert the cushion pad.

# Beautiful bolsters to make

Bolsters are special occasion cushions. Whether you choose a sumptuously opulent Turkish style or a tailored bolster with gathered and buttoned ends, their shapes can mix or match with all styles of furnishing.

### Suitable fabrics

Any closely woven medium or heavy-weight fabric, such as linen, firm tweed or velvet, is suitable for bolsters. Very light-weight or loosely woven fabric like lawn or soft tweed is unsuitable as it will pull at the seams. For bolsters with soft gathered ends choose a supple fabric such as velvet, velours or rayon dupion. For maximum impact choose plain fabrics or fabrics with interesting textures and apply decoration in the form of appliqué bands or braiding. Fabrics with large or one way patterns may be difficult to match at the seams, so take care when choosing these.

Fabric for making the lining should be firm and closely woven. If you choose down and feathers for a filling, use down-proof cambric, whereas calico or cotton sateen are better choices for Terylene fibre or kapok fillings.

▲ *Piped and tasselled bolster*

▲ *Appliqué on a plain bolster*  ▲ *Bolster with decorative ends*

▲ *Turkish bolster with braid*

▲ *Square bolster with patchwork*  ▲ *Plain bolster with huge tassels*

## Turkish bolsters

These are the easiest bolsters to make as the cover simply consists of one piece of fabric seamed down the middle, gathered at both ends and finished with cords or large tassels for decoration. These bolsters are most effective if they are large, soft and colourful.

### You will need

For a Turkish bolster about 11 inches in diameter and 34 inches in length:

- ☐ 1yd 36in wide fabric for the cover
- ☐ 1½yds 36in wide fabric for the lining
- ☐ 4¼lbs feathers and down or 5lb kapok or Terylene fibre for the filling
- ☐ Matching sewing thread, tacking cotton
- ☐ 4 large tassels (you can buy them from a furnishing shop or make your own)
- ☐ 1½yds dressing-gown cord, without tassels
- ☐ Scissors
- ☐ Chalk, string, 13in square of brown paper and drawing pin for making a template

### The lining

Measure and cut the lining fabric into two pieces, a body piece 1yd square and a piece 18 by 36 inches for the ends.

Fold the yard of lining in half, right sides facing, and tack and stitch two 10 inch long seams as shown in figure 1, taking ½ inch seam allowance.

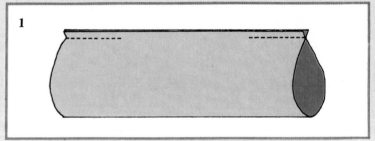

1

Make a circular brown paper template 13 inches in diameter, using the method given on page 8 for the design for circular tablecloths. Then using the template as a pattern, cut 2 circles from the remaining fabric.

Pin and tack one of the circles to one end of the tube of lining fabric, right sides facing, then stitch the circle into place, taking a 1 inch seam allowance. Snip into the seam allowance of the lining tube as shown in figure 2.

2

Repeat for the other end.

Turn the lining right side out, through the opening, and insert the filling. The filled lining should be fairly firm but squashy.

Close the opening firmly with slip stitch.

### The cover

Fold the yard of cover fabric in half, right sides facing, and tack and stitch along the edges as shown in figure 3, taking a ½ inch seam allowance. Press the seam open.

Pin, tack and stitch a $\frac{3}{4}$ inch turned hem at each end of the tube, leaving an opening of 1 inch in each hem (figure 4).

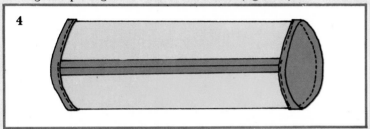

Turn the cover right side out.

Cut the length of dressing-gown cord in half and thread one half through one of the turned hems. Close the 1 inch opening. Pull up the cord so that the end is closed and tie the cord decoratively but firmly. Sew a tassel to each end of the cord (figure 5).

Insert the filled lining into the open end of the cover and finish that end as before.

## Fitted bolster with gathered ends

These bolsters are tailored with a zipped opening in the body and neat gathered ends finished off with self-covered buttons.

### You will need

For a bolster 7 inches in diameter and 17 inches in length:

☐ $\frac{3}{4}$yd 36in wide fabric for the cover
☐ $\frac{3}{4}$yd 36in wide fabric for the lining
☐ Matching sewing thread, tacking cotton
☐ Two 1in diameter button moulds
☐ 15in zip to match the cover fabric
☐ $1\frac{1}{2}$lbs down and feathers or 2lbs kapok or Terylene fibre for filling
☐ Scissors
☐ Chalk, string, 9in square of brown paper and drawing pin for making a template

### The lining

From the lining fabric measure and cut a body piece $26\frac{1}{2}$ inches by 19 inches. The remaining fabric is for cutting 4 circles 9 inches in diameter for the ends.

Make a template from the brown paper (for the method see instructions on page 8) and cut the 4 circles from the lining fabric, using the template as a pattern.

Make up the lining as for the Turkish bolster.

### The cover

Measure and cut out three strips from the cover fabric, one strip $26\frac{1}{2}$ inches long by 19 inches wide for the body, and the other two strips $26\frac{1}{2}$ inches long by 5 inches wide for the ends.

Fold the body piece of the cover fabric in half and pin and tack the edges together taking $\frac{1}{2}$ inch seam allowance. Tack firmly down the full length. Stitch a 2 inch seam at each end (figure 6). Do not remove the tacking but press the full length of the seam open.

Place the closed zip, right side down, over the tacked opening. Tack the zip firmly into place (figure 7). Turn the tube right side out and hand-sew the zip into place using a firm back stitch with only a tiny stitch showing on the surface.

Remove the tacking and turn the cover to the wrong side.

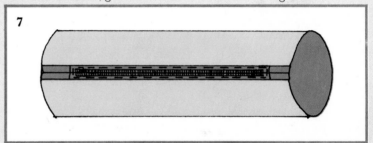

### Buttoned and gathered ends

Take one of the 5 inch strips of cover fabric and fold in half, right sides facing. Tack and stitch the ends together taking a $\frac{1}{2}$ inch seam allowance. Press the seam open and turn right side out. Place the wrong side of the ring of cover fabric to one of the lining circles. Tack and stitch together (figure 8) taking a 1 inch seam allowance. Snip the seam allowance on the cover fabric and make a line of gathering stitches round the top edge of the ring as shown. Draw up these gathers firmly and finish off securely. The ring of fabric is now gathered up so that it lies against the lining circle (figure 9).

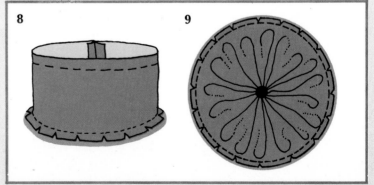

Cover a button mould using remnants of cover fabric and sew the button to the gathered end to cover the centre of the gathering. Make the other end of the bolster in the same way.

Tack and stitch the buttoned ends to the body tube, right sides facing, as shown (figure 2) for the lining of the Turkish bolster.

Turn the cover right side out and insert the filled lining through the opening.

# Bed-heads and spreads

The most eye-catching mass of colour in a bedroom is often the bedspread and if you are lucky enough to own a fine patchwork quilt it can become the focal point of your room. But for just as good an effect it's easy to make an unlined, throw-over bedcover and head-board cover to match.

## Making a bed cover

### Calculating the material

Measure the bed carefully, noting its width and length, also the height from the floor to the top of the bed clothes. (Whether you buy one, two or three lengths depends of course on fabric width and bed size.) Should you decide to tuck the cover around the pillows, it is wise to allow an extra 18in of material on each length. Remember that if the material has a block print you must allow extra in order to match the design at the seam. (Furnishing fabric print designs are usually large block repeats.)

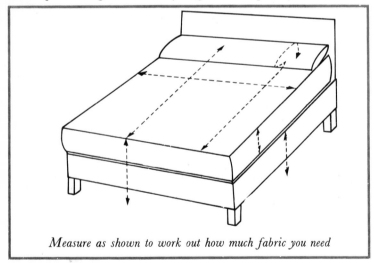

*Measure as shown to work out how much fabric you need*

### To make the cover

Making instructions are given for the average double bed size, for which you will need two lengths of 48in or 54in fabric.

Cut the fabric into two lengths, making sure that they match together if the fabric has a design. Cut one length in half lengthwise, thus making two half widths. Cut off the selvedges so that the material will not cockle. Put the right sides together and tack the two half widths on to each side of the centre panel. Join the pieces with a flat-fell seam.

### Rounded corners

Put the cover over the bed and pin a line where the material touches the floor at the corners of the foot of the bed. Use a

*Decorate an attractive throw-over bed cover with simple embroidery*

large dinner plate or some other rounded object about 18in in diameter as a guide to neaten the curve at the corner. Cut away the excess material leaving a $1\frac{1}{4}$in hem allowance.

Turn in $\frac{1}{4}$in and then make a 1in hem all round the cover. To avoid puckering and fullness at the rounded corners, make a line of running stitches in strong thread $\frac{1}{4}$in from the edge. When you turn in the further inch of material the thread can be pulled up and the fullness evenly distributed. Mitre the corners at the head of the cover and machine or hand-sew the hem.

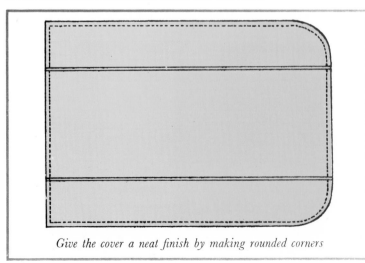

*Give the cover a neat finish by making rounded corners*

*Or save time by buying a pretty printed fabric and sewing on a border*

## Version for bed with footboard

If the bed has a foot-board, a throw-over bed cover will be rather bulky at the corners. To avoid this, simply make the bed-spread as already described but join the half widths along the length of the bed only. But remember to take this into consideration when calculating the amount of fabric you'll need. Also, this time, the tuck-in at the top will have to be longer to wrap completely round the pillows, so allow another 10in for tucking down the back. When making up this version, mitre all the outside corners.

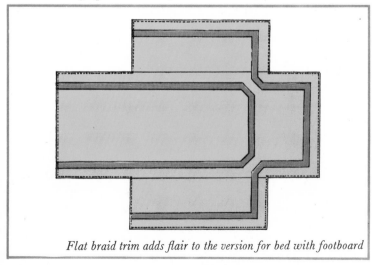

*Flat braid trim adds flair to the version for bed with footboard*

You can trim bed covers when the cover is finished but remember to trim head-board covers before stitching.

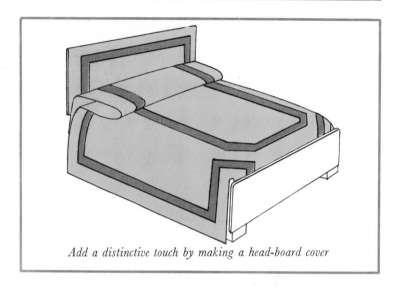

*Add a distinctive touch by making a head-board cover*

## Covering a head-board

First, measure up to find the amount of material you'll need. Measure the height of the head-board, allow twice this amount plus allowance for turnings and hems. For a double bed you will need two lengths. You will also need 1½yds of ½in tape (cut into four pieces) and border trim as required.

### To make up

Join fabric if two widths are required with a flat-fell seam and press. Place fabric right side up, attach and stitch trim. Next, turn in ¼in then make a 1in hem top and bottom on wrong side. Machine or hand sew, attaching the four pieces of tape in positions indicated, measuring from seam edge to centre.

Now fold cover in half with trim on the inside. Stitch the two seams with ¾in turnings.

Press open seams and stitch across corners as shown. This is for ¾in thickness of board. The thickness of the head-board dictates what measure to stitch across corners.

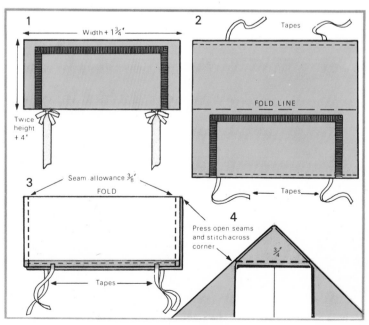

# Crochet goes to bedheads

This beautiful bedhead is a typical example of lacis crochet, which is derived from filet crochet and which originated in Germany. The crochet panel illustrated has been worked in lime green and mounted over foam padding covered in royal blue fabric. Work the panel in a colour to suit your decor.

**Size**
13in deep by 36in long

**Tension for this design**
3sp and 3 rows to 1in over patt worked on No. 1·25 (ISR) crochet hook

**Materials shown here**
Coats Chain Mercer-Crochet No. 20, 4 balls
One No. 1·25 (ISR) Milward crochet hook
Foam padding 13in deep by 36in long by 3in wide
1yd 45in wide fabric
Metal or bamboo rod to fit
Rings 1½in diameter if fabric tabs are not required

## Bedhead in lacis crochet

Using No. 1·25 (ISR) hook make * 4ch, leaving last loop of each st on hook work 2dtr into 4th ch from hook, yrh and draw through all loops on hook, (a 2dtr cluster made), rep from * 40 times more. 41 clusters.

**1st row** 3ch, miss next cluster, 1dtr into base of next cluster, (sp made), *3ch, 1dtr into base of next cluster, rep from * 37 times more, 3ch,

leaving last loop of each st on hook work 3 dtr into base of next cluster, yrh and draw through all loops on hook, (a 3dtr cluster made). Turn. 40sp.

**2nd row** 4ch, 2dtr cluster into 1st cluster, 3ch, 1dtr into next dtr, (sp made over sp), *3dtr into next sp, 1dtr into next dtr, rep from * 37 times more, (38 blocks made over 38 sp), 3ch, 3dtr cluster into next cluster. Turn.

**3rd row** 4ch, 2dtr cluster into 1st cluster, 1 sp, 1dtr into each of next 4dtr, (block made over block), *3ch, miss next 3 dtr, 1dtr into next dtr, rep from * 35 times more, (36 sp made over 36 blocks), 1 block, 3ch, 3dtr cluster into next cluster. Turn.

**4th row** 4ch, 2dtr cluster into 1st cluster, 1 sp, 1 block, 36 sp, 1 block, 3ch, 3dtr cluster into next cluster. Turn.

**5th row** 4ch, 2dtr cluster into 1st cluster, 1 sp, 1 block, 2 sp, *3dtr cluster into next dtr, (4ch, 2dtr cluster into 4th ch from hook) twice, 3dtr cluster into same place as last 3dtr cluster, (diamond cluster made), 1dtr into next dtr, rep from * twice more, 4ch, 2dtr cluster into 4th ch from hook, (cluster bar made), 1dtr into next dtr, 8 sp, 3ch, 3dtr cluster into next dtr, follow diagram to end of row Turn.

**6th row** 4ch, 2dtr cluster into 1st cluster, 1 sp, 1 block, 2 sp, (3ch, 1dc into centre ch of next diamond cluster, 3ch, 1dtr into next dtr) 3 times, 3ch, 1dtr into next dtr, 6 sp, diamond cluster into next dtr, 1dtr into next dtr, diamond

cluster into next cluster, follow diagram to end of row. Turn.

**7th row** 4ch, 2dtr cluster into 1st cluster, 1 sp, 1 block, 2 sp, (diamond cluster into next dc, 1dtr into next dtr) twice, follow diagram to end of row. Turn.

**8th row** 4ch, follow diagram to end of row. Turn.

**9th row** 4ch, 2dtr cluster into 1st cluster, 1 sp, 1 block, 2 sp, diamond cluster into next dc, 1dtr into next dtr, 9 sp, 3ch, 1dc into centre ch

of next diamond cluster, 3ch, 1dtr into next dtr, 1 sp, *miss 2ch, 1dtr into next ch, 1ch, inserting hook from behind last dtr work 1dtr into first of 2 missed ch, (cross made), 1dtr into next dtr, rep from * 3 times more, 1 sp, follow diagram to end of row. Turn.

**10th row** 4ch, 2dtr cluster into 1st cluster, 1 sp, 1 block, 2 sp, 3ch, 1dc into centre ch of next diamond cluster, 3ch, 1dtr into next dtr, 7 sp, diamond cluster into next dtr, 1dtr into next dtr, 2 sp,

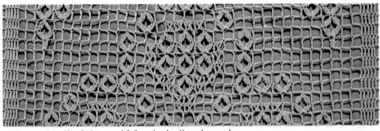

*Close-up detail of the motif for the bedhead panel*

*Diagram for working the lacis crochet bedhead panel*

*Lacis crochet in lime green over royal blue gives a bright, crisp effect for modern bedroom decor*

(diamond cluster into next dtr, miss 2dtr, 1dtr into next dtr, miss 2dtr) twice, diamond cluster into next dtr, (3 diamond clusters made over 4 cross sts), follow diagram to end of row. Turn.

**11th row** 4ch, follow diagram to end of row. Turn.

**12th row** 4ch, 2dtr cluster into first cluster, 1 sp, 1 block, 11 sp, diamond cluster into next dc, 1dtr into next dtr, 1 sp, miss next dtr, 1dtr into next dtr, 1ch, inserting hook from behind last dtr work 1dtr into dtr just missed, (cross st made over cross st), 1dtr into next dtr, follow diagram to end of row. Turn.
Beg each row with 4ch, follow diagram to top, turn diagram and omitting last 2 rows follow diagram back to 1st row. Fasten off.

## To make up

Dampen crochet and pin out to measurements.
Cut fabric for covering foam, noting that ½in has been allowed on all sides for seams.
Cut 2 pieces 14in by 37in for front and back.
Cut 2 pieces 4in by 37in and 2 pieces 4in by 14in for gussets.
Cut 5 pieces 4in by 8in for tabs, if required in place of rings. Fold tab pieces in half lengthwise and st long edges. Turn to RS.
Join 1 long gusset piece to 1 short gusset piece by machine stitching short ends. Join rem 2 gussets in same way. Join 2 sections tog to form rectangle,

machine stitching across free short ends.
Place front section to gussets, RS tog and machine st all round.
Place and tack tabs in position to RS of back section, raw edges tog. Place long edge with tabs to gussets, RS tog and machine st.
Trim seams, turn to RS and insert pad. Turn in rem seam allowance on back section and sl st to gussets.
Sew crochet in place to front of completed pad.

# Bedcover with flounce

The first thing that catches the eye in a bedroom is the bed-spread because it is usually the largest horizontal mass of colour. For this reason, the bedcover should be the first item when you come to plan a new look for your bedroom.

A flounced or box-pleated bed base cover with a throw-over bedspread is as easy to make as a tablecloth, but fabrics need to be carefully chosen. Large, repeat patterns are generally unsuitable because pleats break up the effect of the pattern. Fabrics with a one-way design or small compact prints are best. The instructions given in this chapter show you how to work out the amount of material needed for any size bed.

## How to measure up

**Bed base cover, for the flounce only**—Measure the length and width and allow 3 times each amount (that is, as the diagram shows, 6 times the length plus 3 times the width) times the depth, plus turnings and hem allowance. Remember, you will not need a flounce at the bed-head end.

For lining the base top, measure the length and the width with the mattress removed.

**For the throw-over bed cover** – Measure up as described on page 44. But also remember that you will need less in length and width to allow the bed-base flounce to show. You'll require the same amount for lining.

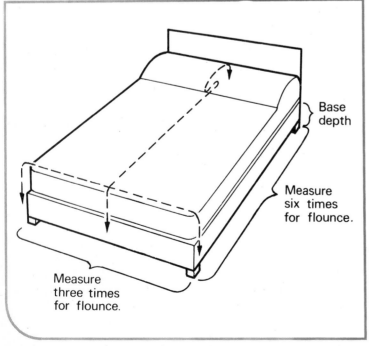

Base depth

Measure six times for flounce.

Measure three times for flounce.

## Box pleating with 4in pleats

In box pleating, the spaces between the pleats are all equal. Following the diagram, pleat B to A and C to D. BC forms the top of the pleat. For an easy method of pleating cut a marker in thick card as the diagram shows.

## Gauging

Gauging is a method by which you can fit a very large amount of material into a small width. Make two rows of running stitches along the top edge of the flounce, each stitch one above the other, as shown in the diagram. The length of the stitch and space depend on the amount of fullness you require.

## Cutting for the flounce

For making the flounce, cut the fabric into strips lengthwise or across the width, as required. The diagram shows you how to cut for a very pronounced one-way design, that is, across the width from selvedge to selvedge.

## To make the bed-base cover

Join the strips for the flounce together in one long piece. If you've used one-way fabric make sure each piece is joined the right way up.

Tack, then machine or hand sew all the seams. Now machine or hand sew a $\frac{1}{2}$in hem down the two sides and around the bottom.

You are now ready either to gauge or box pleat the flounce. For box pleating use the card marker, press and tack, making sure that all seams come under a pleat pressed edge.

Attach the lining top at this stage using a plain seam $\frac{1}{2}$in from the edge. Stitch again, to neaten along the raw edge. With a pleated flounce, make sure two box pleats appear together at the two corners as shown in the diagrams. This forms an inverted pleat.

## To make the throw-over cover

Cut the fabric in two lengths making sure they match, particularly if the fabric has a design. Put the right sides together, tack, then machine or hand sew with a flat fell seam. Press. Now, join the lining using the same method. Press.

Place both fabric and lining together with right sides facing. Now tack and then machine or hand sew $\frac{1}{4}$inch from the edge all round leaving about 18inch at the head-board end open to enable you to turn the whole thing to the right side.

Turn the cover, press the edge and fell opening together. At this stage if you are using a trim or fringe, machine or hand sew the trim all round the edge of the bed cover.

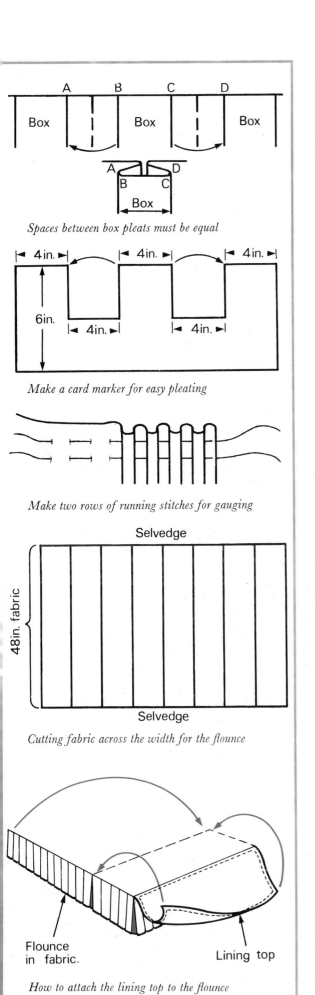

*Spaces between box pleats must be equal*

*Make a card marker for easy pleating*

*Make two rows of running stitches for gauging*

*Cutting fabric across the width for the flounce*

Flounce
in fabric.

Lining top

*How to attach the lining top to the flounce*

# Comfortable continental bedcovers

The modern, simple way to make a bed is to use a continental quilt, or duvet (pronounced doovay), which is teamed with the pillows and linen. You can simplify your bedclothes still further by making a detachable duvet cover which stands in for a bedspread and top sheet and is made like a giant pillowcase. For maximum effect make it from a pretty fabric to match with bottom sheet and pillowcase.

### Suitable fabrics
For making the duvet case use either Terylene or Terylene and cotton mixture sheeting, and for the filling use Terylene wadding. Both sheeting and wadding must be 78 inches wide to give you the length you need without piecing.
For the detachable cover use Terylene, Terylene and cotton, or cotton sheeting in a 90 inch width.
Always use sewing threads appropriate to the fibre content of the fabric.

### Bed sizes
Yardages and making up instructions for both duvet and detachable cover are given for a 4ft 6in double bed size.
For other bed sizes, the fabric required is twice the bed width measurement plus 18 inches in a 78 inch width for the case, and a 90 inch width for the cover.
The amount of wadding needed is equal to the bed width plus 18 inches, in a 78in width. Apart from the double bed size, the making up instructions are for all bed sizes.

## Making the duvet

### You will need
- [ ] 4yds 78in width sheeting
- [ ] Sheet of Terylene wadding 78in by 72in
- [ ] Matching sewing thread
- [ ] Tacking cotton
- [ ] Extra long pins
- [ ] Tailor's chalk
- [ ] Yardstick

Cut the fabric into 2 pieces. If necessary, trim the wadding to the same size (figure 1).
Lay the fabric pieces, right sides facing, on the floor and pin them together down each long side. Tack and machine stitch plain seams $\frac{5}{8}$ inch from the edges (figure 1).

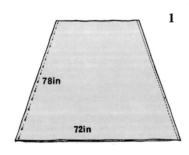

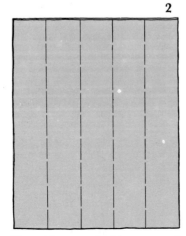

Turn the case inside out and press it. With the tailor's chalk draw 4 straight lines

from top to bottom, making 5 divisions of equal width. Trace tack these lines on each side of the case (figure 2).
Feed the wadding into the case and work it about until it lies flat and even and fills the case snugly (figure 3).

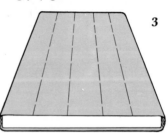

To enclose the wadding, turn in the raw edges at each end of the case to a depth of $\frac{1}{2}$ inch and tack the corresponding edges together. Topstitch by machine (figure 4).

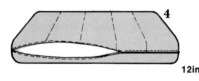

The duvet must now be stitched down the length firmly so that the wadding is kept in place and will drape around your body in bed. Lay it flat on the floor, match up and pin along the trace tacked lines, to include both case and filling (figure 5). Tack along the pinned lines, through all the layers.

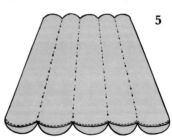

You may be able to machine stitch along the tacked lines if you roll the duvet tightly under

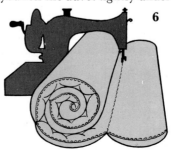

the arm of the machine and have someone help you hold it as you stitch (figure 6).
If this is not possible, sew by hand using long, firm back stitches.
Remove all the tacking threads.

## The detachable cover

### You will need
- [ ] 4yds 90in width sheeting
- [ ] Matching sewing thread
- [ ] Tacking cotton, pins
- [ ] 4yds straight tape

Cut the fabric into 3 pieces (figure 7).

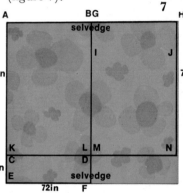

Allow $\frac{3}{4}$ inch for all seams and hems. On the back and turn-in pieces machine stitch turned hems from A to B and from C to D on the wrong side of the fabric (figure 8).

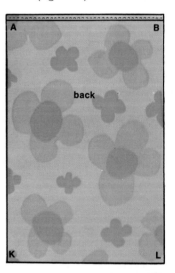

With the right sides of the fabric together, tack and machine stitch the turn-in to

50

the front from EG to FH (figure 9).

Press both seam allowances down together and make a flat-fell seam as described on page 6.

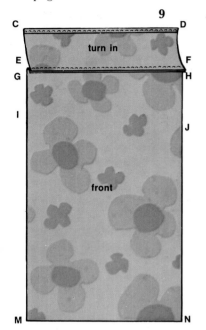

Fold down the turn-in and tack from G to I and H to J (figure 10).

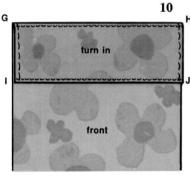

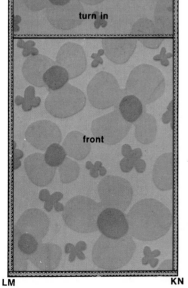

▲ *Continental quilt, or duvet, covered in patterned fabric with pillowcase and bottom sheet to match*

With right sides of the front and back together, make flat fell seams from BEG to LM, AFH to KN and LM to KN (figure 11).

Unless the duvet is tied to the duvet cover it will slip about inside. Sew 6 inch lengths of tape to the duvet as shown (figure 12).

Sew tapes to corresponding points inside the cover so that the stitching is invisible on the right side (figure 13).

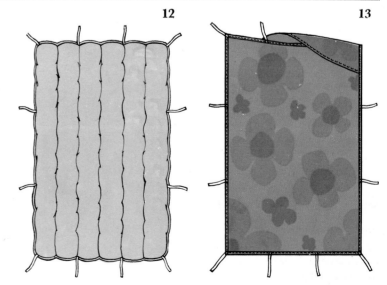

# The art of patchwork

This chapter begins patchwork with the simplest shapes and designs using the hexagon which has six sides.

First decide what you would like to make. A single flower motif is effective on an apron pocket or child's dress. With the hexagon (the easiest template because the angles are large) you could make a pincushion, cushion cover or baby's quilt.

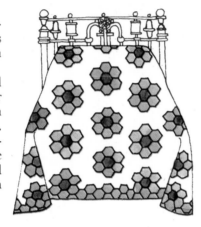

## Preparing for patchwork

Here is a list of the equipment you will need:

**Templates.** Used to make the shapes for the patches. Made from metal or perspex or very stiff card, these are the exact size of the finished patch. When you cut out the fabric, leave a $\frac{3}{8}$in turning allowance round the edge of the template.

**Stiff paper.** This is for the paper shapes which are tacked into the pieces of fabric to hold the patches firm. They should be made from strong brown paper or thin card (glossy magazine covers are ideal). These shapes must be very accurately cut, or the finished patchwork will not lie flat.

**Scissors.** Use a sharp pair to cut out the fabric patches, but use an old pair to cut out the paper shapes so you don't blunt the cutting edge of your good ones.

**Needles.** When stitching together the patches, use a needle as fine as you comfortably can.

*Some simple but effective ways of using hexagon florets*

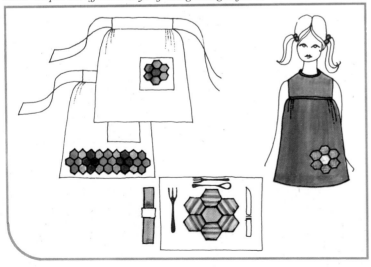

**Thread.** If the patches are made of a fine cotton or linen, use fine cotton to sew them together. For silk patches, use sewing silk. For tacking material to the paper shapes, mercerized cotton is better than tacking cotton as it makes finer holes in the fabric. This is important, since the tacking will stay in for some time.

**Pins.** Use fine steel pins to avoid leaving holes in the fabric.

**Fabric.** Any odd scraps can be used but one thing is very important to remember: don't mix fabrics of different weights in the same piece of work. A strong damask patch can pull a delicate material next to it to pieces. And if the finished article is to be washed, avoid mixing fabrics with different washing methods. Check that a fabric is colour-fast by taking a small piece, wetting it thoroughly and pressing it with a warm iron on to a piece of white material to see if the colour runs. Never use material that may be at all worn, as to repair a worn-out patch is an irritating and laborious job. But this doesn't mean you can never work with a used fabric, dresses that are discarded or out-grown or curtains that shrank in the wash are all usable, but when mixing old and new, wash the new material first to prevent the risk of shrinking afterwards.

If you are working with light-weight fabrics and find that the design needs a material which is so transparent that the turnings show through, use a bonded fibre fabric instead of a paper shape and leave it in the finished work.

## Making the patches

Using the template, carefully cut out the paper shapes. You may prefer to draw round the template before cutting out, but see that the pencil is really sharp and that you always hold it at the same angle. Then, using the template as a guide, cut out the patches, allowing $\frac{3}{8}$in extra for turnings. (If the fabric is creased, press it first.) Try to keep two edges of the template parallel to the grain of the fabric, as this strengthens the patch. Pin the paper shape on to the wrong side of the material and fold over the turnings. Starting with a knot or a back stitch, tack round the patch, using one tacking stitch to hold down each corner. Finish off by making a small extra stitch and take out the pin.

## Joining the patches

Put the right sides of the two patches together and over-sew with tiny stitches along one edge. Start by laying the end of the thread along top of edge and sew over it from right to left. Push the needle through the fabric at right angles to the edge so that the stitches will be neat and the patches won't stretch. To fasten off, work backwards for four stitches. Several patches can be joined continuously, but make sure that the corners are firm by sewing one or two extra stitches over them. You will find it easier to sew together small units first and join up these groups later.

## To finish off

When all the patches are sewn together, press the patchwork on the wrong side with a warm iron. (If you feel that the front of the work needs pressing too, take out the tacking, leave the paper shapes in to prevent the turnings from making a pressing mark and press gently on the right side.) Take out all the paper shapes and tack round the edge of the work from the right side to hold the turnings of the edge patches secure. Press again on the wrong side to remove any marks left by the tacking. Pressing is important at this stage as it helps in subsequent laundering.

## Mounting

The patchwork is now ready to be mounted on to the main article. Pin the patchwork in place and slip-stitch, with tiny stitches, all round. Remove the edge tacking, press lightly just round the edge, and your first patchwork is complete. If the area of patchwork is quite large, catch it to the ground material at various points.

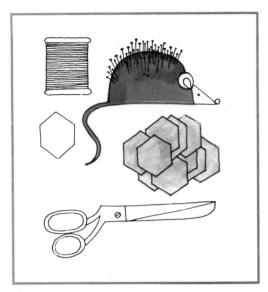

Make baby's quilt with $1\frac{1}{4}$ in patches on broderie
Anglaise: line with washable Terylene ►

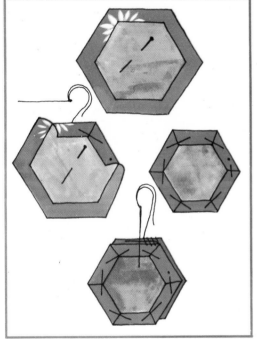

▲ Pin, tack then stitch the patches together
▼ Press the patches on the right side

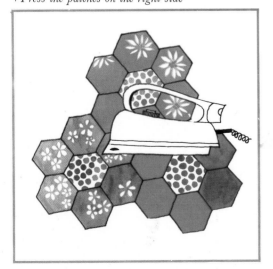

# American patchwork quilt

American patchwork is often closer to appliqué work than traditional English patchwork, while its characteristic quilted background gives American patchwork much of its charm. The patchwork shapes derive from English and Dutch patchwork and also from the Americas themselves. One of the most famous of the latter is the princess feather, as illustrated in figure 1, which is thought to have been inspired by the feathered head-dresses of the Red Indian princesses.

▼ 1. *An American quilt using the princess feather and star patterns*

The star is another traditional American pattern with considerable variations on the basic shape. Two stars are given here—the pointed star and the round star, both of which, like the princess feather, are large motifs and should be used in a lively informal way.

### Assembling the pointed star

A section of this pattern is given full size as a trace pattern (figure 2). You will need 8 of these pieces and 4 of them must be reversed. The pieces are joined together as in traditional patchwork and then oversewn to the background. The assembled star is shown in figure 3.

### Assembling the rounded star

A section of this pattern is again given full size (figure 4). You will need 8 pieces and 4 of them must be reversed. They are joined together along the straight edges as shown in figure 5.

## Making your own quilt

American quilts do not reach to the ground but lie on top of another coverlet. An average single bed size quilt should measure about 62in by 100in and a double bed size quilt about 80in by 100in.

### You will need:

□ Background fabric in a neutral colour or a colour which echoes one of the colours you will use in the patchwork. For the best results choose a firm, closely-woven, heavy-weight cotton.

It is possible to use ready made cotton quilting for the background fabric but the patchwork design and quilting should complement each other either in colour or shape.

□ Tacking thread

□ Brown paper

Fold the background into quarters and mark the fold lines with tacking.

Decide which patchwork shapes you will use for the design and cut out several patterns of each complete motif in brown paper. Arrange a quarter of the design using the paper patterns in one of the marked off quarters of the background fabric. When this looks right, and only the designer of the quilt can tell this, mark the placing for the motifs with further tacking. Mark the other quarters in the same way.

### Making up the patchwork

### You will need:

□ Patterned and coloured fabrics for the patches

□ Matching sewing thread

□ A fine needle

□ Sandpaper (medium-coarse)

□ Scissors to cut the sandpaper

□ Scissors to cut the fabric

□ Tacking thread

Draw or trace the shapes you have chosen on to the smooth side of the sandpaper. Cut the sandpaper shapes out and place them rough side down on to the fabric. The sandpaper will cling to the fabric and help you to cut accurately. Unless you wish to centre a particular part of a patterned fabric, place the sandpaper on the wrong side of the fabric as it may be too abrasive for delicate fibres.

Cut accurately round the edge of each sandpaper pattern leaving $\frac{1}{4}$ inch seam allowance. Remove the sandpaper and turn the seam allowance to the wrong side of each patch. Tack the edges down carefully.

Press well using a pressing cloth.

Assemble all the motifs now so that the patchwork is ready to be applied to the background.

### Assembling the cover

### You will need:

□ The marked-up background fabric

□ Tacking thread

□ Sewing thread to match the patches

□ Prepared patchwork

□ Lining fabric (the same amount as the background fabric). This should be nonslip, medium-weight and colour matched to the background fabric

Tack the assembled patchwork on to the background fabric in the design you have chosen. Sew the patchwork down with tiny oversewing stitches, keeping it as flat as possible.

When the patchwork is sewn down, remove all the tacking threads and press the work carefully.

Place the lining on to the finished cover, right sides together, and stitch round the edges leaving a long opening on one side. Turn the cover right side out through the opening and close with oversewing stitches. Catch the lining fabric to the background fabric all over, with tiny stitches at about 5 inch intervals.

**Interlining.** Traditionally American patchwork quilts were made warmer by the addition of extra layers of fabric (old blankets or sheets) placed between the background fabric and the lining. You can choose to follow tradition or dispense with an interlining altogether. On the other hand, if you are using ready-made quilting the interlining is already built-in. Even so, the quilting will still need to be lined.

**Quilting the cover**

These instructions do not apply to ready-made quiltings.

The quilting may be done on a machine with a simple straight stitch or by hand. If you work by hand use tiny running stitches, using a stabbing technique to ensure that all layers are caught together.

In both cases, use a thread to match the background fabric and work the quilting from the middle of the cover towards the edges.

Make rows of stitches through all the layers in patterned lines round the patchwork. The quilting should echo the pattern of the patchwork but can be quite freely expressed. Figure 6 shows a good example of this.

*6. A traditional star with the quilted background echoing the star shape* ►

*▲2. Trace pattern for a section of the pointed star* **3.** *The pointed star assembled* **4.** *Trace pattern for a section of the rounded star* **5.** *The rounded star assembled*

# Thinking big in hairpin crochet

Many fascinating items can be assembled from strips of hairpin crochet. For a first large-scale project, try this bedspread. The illustration shows a similar hairpin crochet bedspread made in a thicker yarn.

### Size

About 80in by 52in excluding fringe (length and width are easily adapted)

**Tension for this design**
Worked on a Quadframe at full width using 3 balls of yarn together throughout

### Materials shown here

Templeton's H and O
Shetland lace
36 balls
One Quadframe
One medium sized crochet hook

## Strips

Using 3 strands of yarn, make a slip loop and place on right hand upright of Quadframe. Hold yarn behind left side with left hand and remember to keep turning the frame towards the left as you work. Insert the crochet hook into the loop in the centre of the frame and draw the thread through to form a loop on the crochet hook, insert the hook under loop in centre of frame and draw yarn through (2 loops on hook), yrh and draw through both loops, *turn frame to left after passing hook and the loop on it to the back, insert hook into loop and

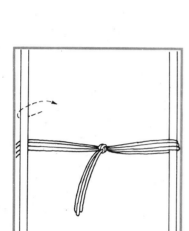
▲ *The first loop on the frame*

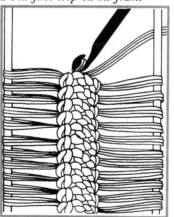
▲ *Working the centre stitch*

draw thread through, insert hook under loop and draw thread through (2 loops on hook), yrh and draw through both loops, rep from * until the frame is full, slip loops off returning the last 2 loops at each side to frame and repeating until strip measures 80in or required length. Fasten off centre thread securely and remove work from frame.
Work another 18 strips or number for width required.

## Joining

Insert crochet hook into first 2 groups of three threads at bottom right hand side of first strip and draw first 2 groups of three threads from bottom of left hand side of 2nd strip through, *draw next 2 groups of three threads from first strip through loop on hook, draw next 2 groups of three threads from 2nd strip through loop on hook, rep from * until all loops are joined. Sew last loop in place.

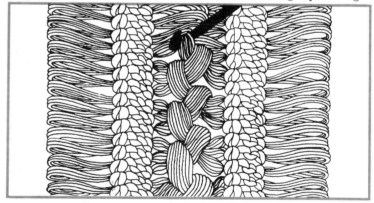
▲ *Joining the strips of hairpin crochet together*

Join other strips together in same way.

## Fringe

Cut lengths of yarn 10in long. Take 6 threads, fold in half and knot into beginning of long side. Work along edge.

## Alternative edging

Work 1 length of hairpin crochet as given for the bedspread until long enough to trim the edges or to reach round bedspread as required.

### Inner edge

Using crochet hook, join double yarn to first loop on right hand side of strip and work *8ch, 1dc into next 3 loops, rep from * to end.

### Outer edge

Using crochet hook, join double yarn to first loop on left hand side, *6ch, into 4th ch from loop work 1dc, 2ch, 1dc into next loop, rep from * to end forming a picot edge.

▼ *Alternative edging for bedspread which could be used instead of the fringe*

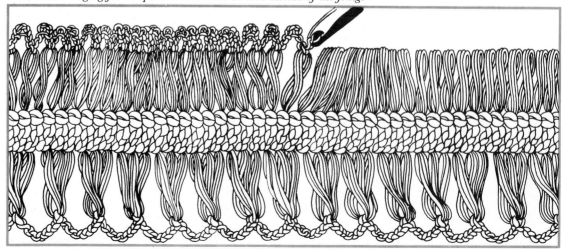

# Symmetry in square motifs

Square motifs can be joined together to make various colourful and practical items, such as this Afghan.

## Size

Afghan of 9 squares by 13 squares, approximately 63in by 91in. One square measures approximately 7in

## Materials shown here

Sirdar Double Knitting
23 balls shade A, Light Blue
21 balls shade B, Mid-Blue
21 balls shade C, Lime yellow
36 balls shade D, Dark Blue
One No.4·00 (ISR) Aero crochet hook

## Note

Each square is worked separately and joined together when all are completed. There are 59 squares worked using D for 1st-3rd rounds, B for 4th-6th rounds and A for 7th-9th rounds, and 58 squares using D for 1st-3rd rounds, C for 4th-6th rounds and D again for 7th-9th rounds.

## Square motif

Using No.4·00 (ISR) hook work 3ch. Join with ss to first ch to form circle.
**1st round** 2ch, work 13tr into circle. Join with ss to 2nd of first 2ch.
**2nd round** 2ch, 1tr between next 2tr, 2tr between each tr to end. Join with ss to 2nd of first 2ch. 28tr.
**3rd round** 4ch, miss 2tr, insert hook round next group of 2tr and work 4tr leaving last loop of each tr on hook, yrh and draw through all 5 loops on hook to form cluster—called 1cl—, 1ch, *1tr between tr of next 2tr group, 2ch, 1cl round next 2tr group, 1ch, rep from * to end. Join with ss to 2nd of first 4ch.
**4th round** Change colour, joining with ss to first ch sp, 3ch, (1tr, 1ch) twice into same sp, (1tr, 1ch) 3 times into each ch sp to end. Join with ss to 2nd of first 3ch.
**5th round** 3ch, 1cl round central tr of 3tr group of previous round, 1ch, *1tr in sp before next 3tr group, 1ch, 1cl round central tr of next 3tr group, 1ch, rep from * to end. Join with ss to 2nd of first 3ch.
**6th round** 2ch, 2tr in first sp, 3tr in each ch sp to end. Join with ss to 2nd of first 2ch.
**7th round** Change colour, joining with ss, 1ch, 1dc in each of next 9tr, 1htr in each of next 3tr, miss 2tr, 5tr in next tr for corner, miss 2tr, 1htr in each of next 3tr, *1dc in each of next 10tr, 1htr in each of next 3tr, miss 2tr, 5tr in next tr for corner, miss 2tr, 1htr in each of next 3tr, rep from * twice more. Join with ss to first ch.
**8th round** 1ch, 1htr into each of next 11 sts, 1tr into each of next 2 sts, work 2tr, 1ch, 2tr all into corner st, 1tr into each of next 2 sts, *1htr into each of next 16 sts, 1tr into each of next 2 sts, work 2tr, 1ch, 2tr all into corner st, 1tr into each of next 2 sts, rep from * twice more, 1htr into each of next 4 sts. Join with ss into first ch.
**9th round** 2ch, 1tr into each of next 15 sts, work 2tr, 1ch, 2tr into corner st, *1tr into each of next 23 sts, work 2tr, 1ch, 2tr into corner st, rep from * twice more, 1tr into each of next 7 sts. Join with ss to 2nd of first 2ch.
Finish off and darn in all ends.

## To make up

Block and press each square lightly under a damp cloth with a warm iron.
Join squares tog using one row of dc worked on the WS, joining alternate colours.

◄ *Detail of the square motif*
*A useful and colourful afghan* ►

# Irish lace bedspread

This superb bedspread shows how Irish lace motifs combine for their full effect. Although such an item in this craft is almost priceless, you may be daunted by so vast a project. If so, use the motifs to make a tray cloth or tablecloth.

**Size**
The bedspread consists of 324 squares, forming 18 rows of 18 squares. Each square is made of one large centre rosebud surrounded by 4 scrolls. 289 small rosebuds fill the spaces at the corner of each square when they are joined.

**Tension for this design**
Each large rosebud measures 2½in x 2½in when unpressed

▼ *A close-up showing in detail the rosebud and scroll motifs*

**Materials shown here**
Coats No.10 Mercer crochet cotton
One No.1·75 (ISR) crochet hook
Each ball of cotton makes 2 large rosebuds, 4 scrolls and 4 small rosebuds

## Large rosebud

Using No.1·75 (ISR) hook make 6ch. Join into a circle with ss into first ch.
**1st round** 5ch, *1tr into circle, 2ch, rep from * 6 times, ending with 1dc into 3rd of first 5ch. (8 sp formed).
**2nd round** Work 4tr in each sp and 1dc in each tr of previous round, ending with 1dc in dc which joined 1st round.
**3rd round** *3ch, 1dc round dc of previous round inserting hook from right to left on the WS of work, rep from * to end, ending with 1dc round last dc of previous round.
**4th round** Work 5tr in each ch sp and 1dc in each dc of previous round, ending with 1dc in last dc of previous round.
**5th round** As 3rd but working 4ch instead of 3 between dc.
**6th round** As 4th but working 6tr instead of 5 into each ch sp.
**7th round** As 3rd but working 5ch instead of 3 between dc.
**8th round** As 4th but working 7tr instead of 5 into each ch sp.
**9th round** As 3rd but working 7ch instead of 3 between dc.
**10th round** Work 2tr, 6dtr, 2tr in each ch sp and 1dc in each dc of previous round, ending with 1dc in last dc. Break yarn and fasten off. Darn in ends.

## Scroll

Using No.1·75 (ISR) hook make 22ch. Join into a circle with a ss into first ch, make another 37ch and join last 22ch into a circle with a ss. Work to and fro on this foundation ch as follows:

**1st row** 1ch, work 1tr into each ch, inc 3 sts after the first 10tr and 3 sts before the last 10tr by working twice into 3ch sts, ending with ss into foundation ch and 1 turning ch. (65 tr).
**2nd row** *1tr, 1ch*, rep from * to * 16 times, rep another 15 times but missing 1 foundation st each time, rep another 17 times without missing any sts, ending with 1ss into last tr, 1ss into foundation ch and 1 turning ch. (48 sp).
**3rd row** *Work 2tr into first sp, 1tr into tr of previous row, 1tr into next sp, 1tr into tr of previous row*, rep from * to * but working 2tr into each of the 15 centre sps, *at same time* when working the 3rd row, after the first 18tr, join with a ss to the centre of one of the rosebud petals. Before working the last 18tr, join scroll to the next petal in the same way. Work 6 more tr and join ends of scroll together by working ss to the corresponding tr at the beg of the row, *2tr, join with ss to corresponding tr, rep from * once more, work to end of row in patt. (126 tr).
When working the last row of the 2nd scroll, make the first join to the next petal of the rosebud, work 6tr and join to the first scroll with a ss in the corresponding tr, *work 3tr on 2nd scroll, join to the first scroll with a ss, rep from * once more, continue working in patt and complete as for first scroll. Join 3rd scroll to rosebud and 2nd scroll in same way. When working the last row of the 4th scroll, it will be joined to both the 3rd and first scrolls. Join to the 3rd scroll as given for the joining of the 2nd and 3rd scrolls, then work 65tr and join in same way to corresponding tr on first scroll. Complete as for previous scroll. Darn in ends. When all the squares have been completed and sewn tog, fill the spaces with small rosebuds as illustrated.

▲ *Despite the pattern being relatively simple to do, not many people attempt such a project and its rarity can make a bedspread like this very valuable*

## Small rosebud

Using No.1·75 (ISR) hook make 4ch. Join into a circle with ss into first ch.
**1st round** 5ch, *1tr into circle, 2ch, rep from * twice, ending with 1dc in 3rd of first 5ch. (4 sp formed).
**2nd round** Work 5tr in each sp and 1dc in each tr of previous round, ending with 1dc in dc which joined 1st round.
**3rd round** *4ch, 1dc in dc of previous round inserting hook from right to left on the WS of work, rep from * to end, ending with 1dc in last dc of previous round.
**4th round** *Work 2tr, 2dtr in ch sp, join petal to centre of scroll with ss, 2dtr, 2tr in same sp, 1dc in dc of previous round, rep from * to end. Fasten off. Darn in ends.

## To make up

Press each piece under a damp cloth with a warm iron. Join squares where edges of scrolls touch using either a needle or a crochet hook.
**Work edging.** *1tr, 4ch, 1tr inserting hook into tr just worked, miss 2 foundation sts*, rep from * to * round all edges. Join with a ss to first tr. Fasten off. Darn in all ends.
Press.

61

# Tied back for elegance

Straight or shaped, tie-backs can be country-style pretty or elegantly formal. Straight braid or straight, covered tie-backs are suitable for simple, light curtains of any length. Shaped tie-backs in matching curtain fabric look best on curtains over eight feet in length where there is sufficient fabric in the curtain to drape in lovely, soft folds into the tie-back.

## Straight tie-backs

These are made from either straight braid or matching curtain fabric. Braid tie-backs are more suitable for light or loosely woven curtains where the fabric is not strong enough for covering the tie-backs.

### Measuring up

Using a glass fibre or fabric tape measure, loop it round the curtain as if it were a tie-back. Do not make the loop so small that it crushes the curtain fabric or so loose that the curtains do not hang well. The loop measurement is the length of the finished tie-back.

The length of the tie-back will depend on the width and the weight of the curtain and you will find that wide, heavy curtains will need a longer tie-back than narrow or sheer curtains.

### You will need

For two tie-backs:
- ☐ ¼yd matched curtain fabric
  or
- ☐ Straight braid 2½in wide to the length required for the two tie-backs plus 1in for turning allowance

- ☐ ¼yd of 27in wide heavy buckram
- ☐ ¼yd 36in wide interlining (medium-weight bonded-fibre fabric)
- ☐ ¼yd 48in wide lining fabric (cotton sateen)
- ☐ Matching sewing cotton, strong linen thread, tacking cotton
- ☐ 4 brass curtain rings, 1 to 2in diameter
- ☐ 2 cup hooks or decorative hooks

### Making a straight tie-back

The curtain fabric or braid, and lining fabric must be 2½ inches wide and ½ inch longer than the required length for the tie-back.

The interlining and buckram must be 2 inches wide and the same length as the finished tie-back.

Measure and cut the curtain fabric or braid, interlining, buckram and sateen lining to required lengths and widths.

Cut each end of each strip into a 'V' shape. To make this shape, on the strips of curtain fabric or braid, and sateen lining measure 1 inch from each end, and on the interlining and buckram measure ¾ inch from each end (figures 1 and 2).

Lay the interlining onto the wrong side of the strip of curtain fabric or braid. Lay the buckram onto the interlining and tack them all firmly together (figure 3).

Fold the edges of the curtain fabric or braid over the buckram and sew them down with large herringbone stitches lacing across the buckram (figure 4).

▲ *Brighten up a plain light-weight curtain with a pretty braid tie-back*
▼ *A selection of beautiful braids suitable for straight tie-backs*

Press carefully using a damp cloth or steam iron.

Turn under the edges of the sateen lining strip $\frac{3}{8}$ inch all round and press carefully with a damp cloth or a steam iron. Lay the sateen onto the buckram, wrong sides facing, and slip stitch it into place round the edges.

Sew a brass curtain ring onto each end of the tie-back (figure 5), using strong linen thread and a firm buttonhole stitch.

Make the other tie-back in the same way.

## Shaped tie-backs

Shaped tie-backs look best on long, heavy curtains. They are made from the same fabric as the curtains and are interlined and stiffened with buckram.

### Measuring up

Measure for the length of the tie-back as before and then halve this measurement.

### Making a pattern

The pattern is for half the tie-back and will be placed onto the folded fabric. Ideas for various shapes for tie-backs are given in figure 6. The length of line A in each shape must be equal to half the measurement of the finished tie-back.

For pattern making you will need:
- Newspaper
- Sheet of brown paper about 30in by 12in
- Pencil
- Scissors

Draw the required shape onto the newspaper, making sure that the measurements and proportions are correct and that the shape is even.

When you are quite satisfied with the shape, transfer it to the brown paper and cut it out very carefully.

### Making a shaped tie-back

For each tie-back you will need:
- Matching curtain fabric. To calculate the amount required lay the pattern onto a folded sheet of newspaper with 3 inches clearance all round (figure 7), and measure it up

- Buckram, interlining and sateen lining, measured as for the curtain fabric
- Matching sewing cotton, strong linen thread and tacking cotton
- Pins
- 2 brass curtain rings, 1 to 2in diameter
- 1 cup hook or decorative hook
- Rubber solution glue
- The paper pattern

Fold the curtain fabric in half along the grain, right sides facing, and lay the brown paper pattern onto it with the centre line of the pattern to the fold of the fabric (figure 7).

Cut out the shape leaving a 3 inch turning allowance. Use the pattern again and cut out the sateen lining in the same way but leave a turning allowance of 1 inch only.

Lay the pattern onto the folded buckram and cut out round the edge of the pattern (no turning allowance) and repeat with the interlining.

Lay the interlining onto the wrong side of the curtain fabric and lay the buckram onto the interlining. Tack them all together as shown in figure 8.

Turn the edges of the cover fabric over the buckram (3 inch turning allowance) and carefully stick them down with a little rubber solution glue. Do not use too much glue and do not pull the curtain fabric too tightly over the buckram as it should 'give' slightly when the tie-back is bent into its finished shape.

It will be necessary to snip into the turning allowance on the curves to help the fabric to lie flat.

Turn in the edges of the sateen lining (take $\frac{1}{8}$ inch over the 1 inch turning allowance) snipping into the turning on the curves where necessary. Press carefully with a damp cloth. Lay the sateen lining onto the buckram, wrong sides facing, and slip stitch into place round the edges.

Sew a brass curtain ring to each end of the tie-back (figure 9), using strong linen thread and buttonhole stitch.

Make the other tie-back in the

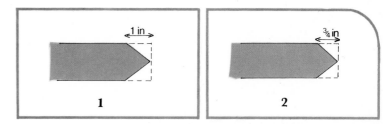

1

2

3

4

5

6

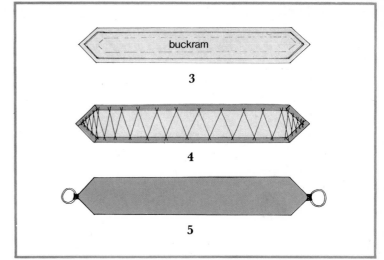

7

8

9

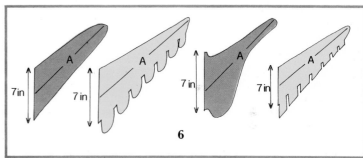

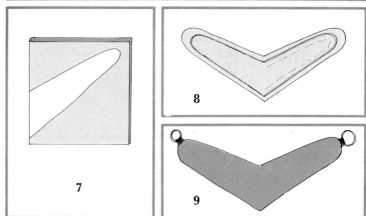

same way.

## Tying back the curtains

Insert a hook into either wall or window frame at each side of the window. To decide the position and height of each hook, place a tie-back round one curtain at different heights and adjust it until it looks right. Make sure that the hook is firmly fixed into the wall as it

will be carrying both the weight of the curtain and the tie-back.

Slip one ring of the tie-back over the hook and loop the tie-back round the curtain, lifting the curtain slightly and arranging the folds so that they gently curve into the tie-back. Slip the other ring over the hook.

Repeat with the other curtain.

# Making unlined curtains

Window curtains can work magic in the home—bringing a touch of brilliant colour to rooms which are dark or diffusing the harsh light of others. Problem windows can have their problems solved, or a room can be given a special character, with imaginative use of fabrics and window fittings. This chapter shows how to plan and make unlined curtains.

### Making up sheers and nets

As these fabrics come in very wide widths, there is no need for widths to be seamed together. Selvedges are usually very neat on these fabrics and side hems are unnecessary but all sewing should be finished off with a double back stitch to prevent the stitches coming undone. Use a special lightweight heading tape for gathering up.

*The modern look: unlined, translucent semi-sheer curtains* ▼

## What you need to know

### How to measure for curtain track

Before buying fabric for curtains, install curtain track on all windows to be curtained. Not only will your curtains look more professional hung from curtain track but they will wear better as well. Expanding wire is not at all satisfactory (except possibly for nets, although even these look more elegant on a track).

Curtain tracks should extend the width of the window plus 6 inches each end, so that the curtains can be drawn back off the window to give maximum daylight. If the curtains are to overlap in the centre, two sections instead of one continuous piece are required and 4 extra inches should be allowed on the length of each of the sections. Curtain track can be bought by the foot and each length of track will require two stops, to fix to the ends, which prevent the curtain hooks from running off.

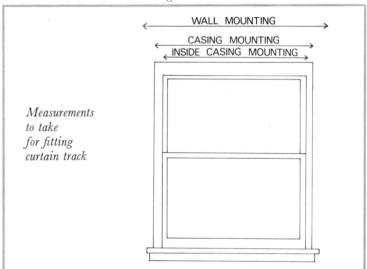

*Measurements to take for fitting curtain track*

### Types of curtain tapes and hooks

The gathering and pleating of curtains is made easier by using the gathering tapes available in the shops. There are several different types available—some produce a soft gather, others deep formal pleats. The tape which produces soft gathers is designed to gather up approximately a double width of material. The more formal pleating tapes gather up as much as three times the fullness of material. Curtain hooks are available in both metal and nylon and are very similar in design and application. Most curtain tracks have their own range of hooks.

### Which fabrics for unlined curtains

Unlined curtains show to best advantage with light filtering through them, and good fabrics for this are coarsely woven linen and Dralon semi-sheers. Some of the brilliantly patterned fabrics look even better with the light behind them but it may be necessary to have a second, lightweight curtain close to the window if privacy at night is necessary. Furnishing fabrics usually measure between 48 and 50 inches wide, while sheers and nets come in widths from 36 inches wide up to 120 inches wide.

### How much fabric to buy

Measuring up for the amount of curtain material you require need not hold any fears. It is a matter of simple mathematics. First, measure for the width of fabric needed. Measure the length of the curtain track and multiply by two (for double fullness). To this, add a sum of inches for an allowance for side hems, usually two inches on each side of each curtain. Add a further 6 inches to each curtain width if they are to overlap in the centre. The total is the width of fabric needed for the *pair* of curtains. For windows measuring more than 4 feet wide, it is necessary to join widths of material to achieve the overall width necessary for gathering. The chart shows the number of widths you will need for different sized windows.

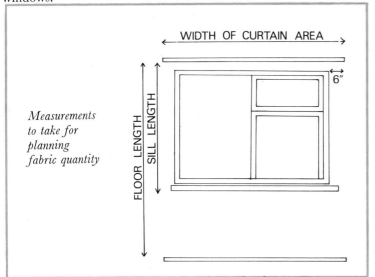

*Measurements to take for planning fabric quantity*

WIDTH OF CURTAIN AREA

FLOOR LENGTH

SILL LENGTH

6"

## Widths of fabric required

| Width of curtain area | Number of widths required per curtain (for simple gathered head) |
|---|---|
| 4′ 6″ and under | 1 |
| 4′ 6″—5′ 6″ | 1½ |
| 5′ 6″—7′ 6″ | 1½ |
| 7′ 6″—10′ 0″ | 2 |

### How to measure for length

Using a steel tape or a yardstick, measure the curtain length from the curtain track to either the window sill or the floor (see diagram). To this measurement, add 6 inches for a double 3 inch hem at the bottom and add 2½ inches for the heading.

This measurement, multiplied by the number of widths required will give you the length of material required for a pair of curtains. If you decide upon a pattern with a large repeat, extra fabric will have to be allowed for matching. Widths seamed together must match as to pattern and all the windows in the room must match. The shop assistant will help you when you have chosen your fabric but for a general rule of thumb, you will need an extra pattern repeat on each curtain length: eg (see diagram) for three curtain widths, allow three extra pattern repeats.

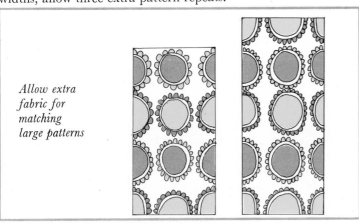

*Allow extra fabric for matching large patterns*

## Making up curtains

### Cutting and seaming

Place the fabric on a large, flat surface for cutting—the floor is ideal if you haven't a large table. Make one end absolutely straight by drawing a thread and cutting along the line. Measure and mark with pins for the first width. Fold the material along the line marked with pins and cut along the fold. Match up the pattern if necessary, and cut off the second width in the same way. Continue until all the widths are cut.

If it is necessary to cut half a width, for curtains taking ½ widths for instance, fold a width lengthwise, and cut along the fold. Cut selvedges off both edges and join widths (and half widths), using a flat fell seam. Use a loose tension and a long stitch for machining the seams.

### Sewing unlined curtains

Unlined curtains require a good hem at the sides to prevent them from curling back. Fold over one inch and then another inch, pin and tack and then machine the side hems or hand stitch using a loose blanket stitch, (each stitch about ¼ inch apart).

Turn up 3 inches and then another 3 inches on the bottom hem and stitch by hand, using a loose blanket stitch.

Turn the top edge of the curtain over 2½ inches and make a tacking line 1½ inch down from the folded edge. Cut a strip of gathering tape the width of the curtain plus 2 inches for turnings. Pull out the cords from the part of the tape to be turned under and pin and tack the gathering tape to the curtain along the line of tacking. Turn the ends of the tape under and tack along the bottom edge of the tape. If you are machining the tape to the curtain, machine both edges in the same direction to prevent any drag in the stitching which would show on the finished curtain.

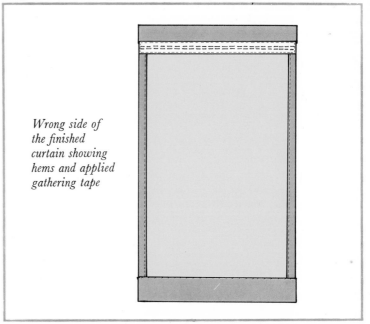

*Wrong side of the finished curtain showing hems and applied gathering tape*

### Gathering curtains

Secure the cords at each of the tape by knotting them together or stitching them securely. Draw the cords up from the middle of the tape and ease the fabric so that it is evenly gathered and the correct width for the window. Knot the cords in the middle and catch them to the tape with one or two little stitches to prevent the knot from hanging down.

The advantage of gathering from the middle is that the gathers are easily released by cutting these little stitches and undoing the knot when the curtains need cleaning or laundering.

# Underlining elegance

Well-lined curtains give a room a warm feeling of luxury. Linings make curtains hang well, they help to insulate the room, and they prolong the life of the curtains by protecting them from fading and rotting. Curtains made from velvet, brocade, silk satin, chintz or man-made fibres should be lined. These fabrics need to be protected from sunlight and always hang better when they are lined.

Laundering lined curtains used to be a problem but now, thanks to lining tapes, you can make curtains with easily detachable linings. This chapter shows how to make linings for curtains with gathered heads, but you will find that exactly the same principle applies to the other headings covered in following chapters.

## Choosing fabric for lining

Traditionally, curtain linings are made from fine cotton sateen in a neutral colour. The neutral colour blends well with almost all curtain fabrics and the lining fabric itself, although light-weight, is closely woven and firm enough to protect the curtains without being too bulky.

Lining fabric is sold in 48 inch widths and it is worth buying one which is pre-shrunk: if it is not, you must allow an extra 6 inches on each yard for shrinkage.

If you decide to buy lining in a colour to match the curtains, look for a fabric which has the same qualities as fine cotton sateen. It is possible to line curtains with fabric other than cotton sateen but, for really successful results, make sure that it is fairly light in weight, very closely woven and, preferably, pre-shrunk.

## Measuring up for lined curtains with a standard heading

A standard heading is a gathered heading. Measure the windows as shown for unlined curtains, and calculate the amount of curtain fabric. You will need the same amount of lining fabric, but without the allowance for headings or for pattern repeats.

## Your shopping list

☐ Curtain fabric
☐ Pre-shrunk lining fabric
☐ Standard heading tape. This is the same as gathering tape, and the yardage required is equal to the width of the ungathered lining, plus 2 inches
☐ Lining tape. Lining tape is specially made for detachable linings and is a double tape with draw cords on one side. Yardage required: the width of the ungathered lining, plus 3 inches
☐ Metal or nylon curtain hooks
☐ Thread to match the curtain fabric
☐ Thread to match the lining fabric
☐ Cord tidy. You will need one cord tidy for each lining and you can purchase this with the heading tape. An empty cotton reel or similar shape cut from cardboard does the same job.

# Headed curtains with detachable linings

## Making the curtains

Measure out, cut and make the curtains in the same way as for unlined curtains, but if joining widths or half widths instead of using flat-fell seams, use plain seams and press open.

Turn up the hems to the required length, stitch on the standard heading tape and gather up the curtains to the required width.

## Making detachable linings

Remember that the linings should be the same size as the curtains without the heading allowance.

Measure out and cut the curtain linings. Join widths, or half widths where necessary, with plain seams and press open.

If the selvedges are tight, snip them every 4 inches. Make good side hems by folding over one inch and then another inch. Tack and machine the side hems. Do not sew the top and bottom hems.

## Attaching the lining tape

To prepare the tape, pull free 1½ inches of the draw cords at one end and knot the cords firmly. Trim off the surplus tape to within ¼ inch of the cord (figure 1).

Fold under ½ inch of the knotted raw end and machine across the fold, stitching right through the tape to secure the knotted cords. With the right side of the lining fabric and the corded side of the lining tape facing you, slip the top raw edge of the lining between the two sides of the tape (figure 2) leaving 1 inch of tape free at the prepared end.

Pin and tack the lining into position. The under side of the tape is slightly wider than the upper side to ensure that the stitching will go through the underside even though it is out of sight while you are stitching the tape on.

Fold over the surplus tape, at the prepared end, level with the side hem edge of the lining, to give a neat edge. Machine the tape to the lining, finishing the unprepared end in the same way as before but leaving the cords free for gathering. Knot the loose ends to prevent them disappearing back into the tape (figure 3).

Gather up the lining to match the gathered curtain and wind the surplus cord of the lining tape on to the cord tidy. Attach the cord tidy to the lining tape with a safety pin. This will keep the cord neat and if you attach the cord tidy to the inside of the lining it will not show when the curtains are hung.

## Attaching the linings to the curtains

With the wrong sides of curtain and lining together, insert the curtain hooks through the buttonholes at the top of the lining tape, then through the pockets in the standard heading tape on the curtain before turning the hooks into their final positions. Both the curtains and their linings will then hang from the same hooks (figure 5).

## Finishing the lined curtains

Hang the lined curtains from the curtain rail and mark the correct length of the linings with a row of pins. The linings should be ½ inch shorter than the curtains. Take down curtains and detach linings. On each lining, unwind the cord from the cord tidy and pull out the gathers. Lay the lining on a large flat surface and turn up the hem to the line of pins. Sew the hem by hand, as described on the previous page.

Attach the finished linings to the curtains again and re-hang. Check that the linings are the correct length.

For a perfectly finished straight hem you must take this much care. It is possible to finish the hem without detaching the lining and taking the gathers out but unless you are very careful indeed you may find the hem hangs crookedly.

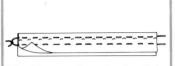

**▲ 1.** *Knot cords and trim lining tape at one end.*

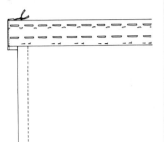

**▲ 2.** *Pin and tack the tape*

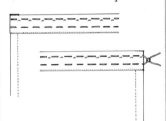

**▲ 3.** *Neaten tape one side, free cords at the other*

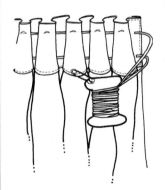

**▲ 4.** *Wind surplus cord on to a cord tidy*

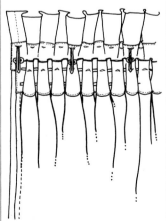

**▲ 5.** *Attach hooks to lining and curtain*

*Make luxurious lined curtains and make them practical with detachable linings* ▼ ▲

# High fashion headings

Curtain headings are as important as the curtains themselves. The way curtains hang depends on the type of heading you choose, and there's no need to hide a curtain heading behind a pelmet—it can be an interesting and integral part of a pretty curtain. Both of the attractive headings given in this chapter look their best on lined curtains, and they also look well with curtain poles—which are back in fashion again. They can lend elegance to a traditional room or give a modern room an exciting look.

▼ *Traditional brass curtain pole encircled with brass curtain rings*

## Pleated headings—pencil pleats

For pencil pleats use a deep heading tape made for this purpose. Pencil pleats are tall and regular at the top, falling smoothly to the bottom of the curtain and need no pelmet (figure 1).

### Measuring up

For curtains with a pencil pleat heading you must allow for at least 2½ times the width of the curtain track. The chart here will help you to calculate how much fabric is needed. You will need as much heading tape as the width of the top of the unpleated curtain.

| Width of curtain track | Number of widths, 48 in wide, required per curtain |
| --- | --- |
| 4′ 6″ and under | 1½ |
| 4′ 6″—5′ 6″ | 2 |
| 5′ 6″—7′ 6″ | 2½ |
| 7′ 6″—10′ 0″ | 3 |

To calculate the length for each width, measure as shown in the instructions on page 64, but allow 5 inches for the heading and 4 inches for the hem.

When you are buying curtain fabric check that it is pre-shrunk: if it is not you must allow for shrinkage.

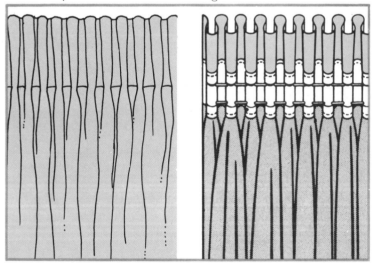

**1.** *Left: pencil pleats seen from the front. Right: the special deep heading tape drawn up, sewn from the back*

### Making up

Make up the curtains and sew on the heading tape, which you will have already measured.

When drawing up the cords on the heading tape, pack all the fullness of the fabric to one end then spread out the pleats carefully to the required width. The pleats will form crisply and evenly. If you are using detachable linings, this is the correct stage at which to attach them.

## Pinch pleats

For pinch pleats use a pleating tape. Pinch pleats are crisp and formal. Single, double or triple pleats are evenly grouped along the top of the curtain and look very decorative without a pelmet. Pinch pleats are formed by using special 4-pronged hooks which are bought with the pleating tape. The prongs of the hooks are inserted into pockets in the tape.

For single pleats put the 2 centre prongs into 2 alternative pockets. For double pleats put 3 prongs into 3 alternative pockets. For triple pleats insert 4 prongs into 4 alternative pockets (figure 2).

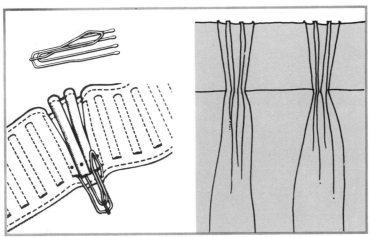

**2.** *Top left: special 4-pronged hook for pinch pleats. Bottom left: hook inserted in the tape for triple pleats. Right: triple pinch pleats*

### Measuring up

Most manufacturers will supply a quantities chart on request. This is essential to help you decide the number of widths and the amount of pleating tape you will need.

Measure for curtain length as shown for unlined curtains, but allow $5\frac{1}{8}$ inches for the heading and 4 inches for the hem.

Pleat up the tape in the arrangement you have chosen and check that the finished length of the pleated tape is the correct length for the curtain track. It may be necessary to re-arrange the pleats to achieve the best effect.

Take out the hooks and mark the pockets you are going to use. Allow $\frac{1}{2}$ inch at each end of the tape for turnings.

### Attaching pleating tape

Make up as for unlined curtains.

Make a $5\frac{1}{8}$ inch hem at the top edge of each curtain. Neaten the ends of the tape by taking $\frac{1}{2}$ inch turnings. Pin and tack the pleating tape to the inside top edge of the curtain, with the top edge of the pleating tape flush with the top edge of the curtain and the pocket openings at the bottom of the tape facing you. Stitch on the tape taking care to avoid the pocket openings.

Insert the hooks in the chosen arrangement and hang the curtains. If you are using detachable linings slip the buttonholes in the lining tape over the pronged hooks.

## Curtains for curtain poles

Curtain poles are the oldest form of curtain track, and there are many types of poles to choose from, both in traditional and modern styles.

A curtain pole replaces a track, and measurements are taken for a pole in exactly the same way as a track. The pole should extend across the window with at least 6 inches extra at each side. The poles are usually supplied with curtain rings and curtain hooks are attached to these rings. Any heading, from a simple gathered type to the more sophisticated pinch pleat heading can be used with a curtain pole.

To use a pleated or gathered heading with a curtain pole simply slot the curtain hooks into the base of each ring on the pole. The advantage of using a heading tape as well as the rings on the pole is that the pleating or gathering is even and the headings are crisp and straight.

*Modern Kirsch rods have mock rings which glide smoothly along a channel, and show off triple pinch pleats handsomely (Fabric by Sanderson)* ►

# Pelmets and curtain valances

A pelmet does not merely hide the curtain track or curtain heading, it can help to balance the proportions of an oddly shaped window. A pelmet will widen a narrow window or link two small ones, give more height to a **wide, shallow window or** beautify a plain one. A valance does a similar job to a pelmet and lends a softer line to a window. This chapter gives some variations.

## Pelmets

A pelmet is a length of fabric, stiffened, cut to a chosen shape and attached to a pelmet board or rail. The pelmet board should be 4 to 6 inches deep and, whether you use a board or a rail, it should extend at least 2 inches beyond each end of the curtain track.
Pelmets are usually attached to pelmet boards with tacks but the method given in this chapter uses touch and close fastening which is easy to apply and does away with unsightly tack heads.
Pelmets are attached to pelmet rails with curtain hooks.

### Suitable fabrics
Most curtain fabrics are suitable for pelmets, with the exception of very light or loosely woven fabrics. If your curtains are very light then a valance made in the same fabric would be more effective than a pelmet.

### Measuring up
Measure round the outside edge of the pelmet board or rail, from the wall at one end to the wall at the other end. This measurement is the exact length of the finished pelmet.
The depth of the pelmet and its shape are a matter of personal choice. Ideas for various shapes are given in figures 1 to 5

▲ **1.** *Plain and simple pelmet*

▲ **2.** *Pelmet with squared ends*

▲ **3.** *Gently curved pelmet*

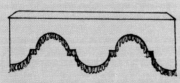
▲ **4.** *Fringe trimmed pelmet*
▼ **5.** *Scalloped pelmet*

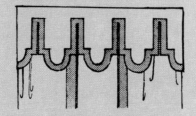

for you to copy. Once you have chosen the shape you want, the depth is so much a matter of proportion that it can only be finalised at the pattern making stage.

### Making a pattern
You will need:
☐ Brown paper. Make sure that you have enough to accommodate the full length and depth for the finished pelmet
☐ Several large sheets of newspaper
☐ Pencil
☐ Ruler
☐ Scissors

Make a preliminary pattern from the newspaper.
If the newspaper sheets are not large enough to accommodate the finished size of the pelmet, join them together with cellophane tape. Measure off the length for the pelmet on the paper, then draw in the shape you have chosen for the pelmet to the depth required. If you have chosen a curved shape, use a suitably sized tin lid or other curved object, such as a plate, as a template for the curves.
Cut out the shape and check that the proportions are correct for the window by sticking it temporarily into position with cellophane tape.
When you are satisfied that the shape and proportions are correct, transfer the shape to the brown paper and cut it out.

### Making the pelmet
You will need:
☐ The brown paper pattern
☐ Covering fabric. To find out how much you will need, measure the length of the paper pattern and the depth at the deepest point and add 1½ inches all round
☐ Lining fabric (cotton sateen)
☐ Buckram for stiffening
☐ Bonded fibre fabric for interlining
(The previous three items are measured as for the covering fabric)
☐ Matching sewing cotton, tacking cotton

☐ Scissors
☐ Rubber solution glue
For attaching the pelmet to a pelmet board you will need:
☐ Touch and close fastening, the same length as the finished pelmet
or, for attaching to a pelmet rail:
☐ Standard curtain heading tape, the same length as the finished pelmet, and curtain hooks

Pin the pattern to the buckram and cut out the buckram round the edge of the pattern. Remove the pattern and cut out the bonded fibre fabric interlining in the same way.
Pin the pattern to the covering fabric and cut out the fabric leaving a 1½ inch turning allowance. Remove the pattern, pin it to the lining fabric, and cut out the lining with a ½ inch turning allowance.
Lay the interlining onto the wrong side of the covering fabric and lay the buckram onto the interlining. Tack all three together and then turn the edges of the covering fabric over the buckram, snipping into the curves and corners where necessary. Secure the covering fabric turnings to the buckram with a little rubber solution glue. Remove the tacking.

### The lining
Turn under the edges of the lining for ¾ inch. Press carefully.

**For attaching a pelmet to a pelmet board.** Separate the two halves of the touch and close fastening and stitch the hooked length along the top edge of the turned in lining, about ¼ inch down on the right side. Machine stitch all the edges of the touch and close fastening or hand-sew with a firm hem stitch. Then lay the lining onto the pelmet, wrong sides facing, and hem stitch into place round the edges.
**For hanging a pelmet from a pelmet rail.** Stitch a length of standard curtain heading tape along the length of the top edge of the turned in

*A pretty gathered valance in country cottage style*

lining $\frac{1}{4}$ inch down on the right side. Finish lining the pelmet as before.

**Hanging the pelmet**
**For a pelmet board.** Take the remaining length of touch and close fastening (the looped side) and stick this along the pelmet board, flush with the top edge, with a very strong glue. When this is dry, simply press the pelmet into place matching the two halves of the touch and close fastening.
**For a pelmet rail.** Insert the hooks into the heading tape

and hang the pelmet as if it were an ungathered curtain.

## Valances

A valance is just like a very short curtain and is hung from a pelmet rail with curtain hooks. Valances can either be gathered or pleated as with curtain headings, so although you measure the pelmet rail in the same way as for pelmets, the measurement will be for the final gathered length. Decide on the depth you want the

valance to be then calculate the amount of fabric necessary in the same way as you would for making unlined curtains, or for pleated headings, as shown on page 68.
For a uniform look match the valance to the curtains in both fabric and style and use the same type of curtain heading tape for both the curtains and the valance. Figures 6 and 7 will give you ideas for styles. Make the valance as you would an unlined curtain, or if you wish to line the valance use the technique for lining pelmets.

▲ 6. *Pencil pleated valance*

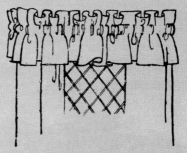

▲ 7. *Simple gathered valance*

# Crocheted door curtain

Door curtains revive the charm of yesterday's furnishings and this one is designed with a motif to suit both traditional and modern decors. The same pattern can be used for a bedspread.

**Measurements**
One motif measures approximately 12in sq

**Tension for this design**
8tr and 4 rows to 1 in worked on No.1·75 (ISR) crochet hook

**Materials shown here**
**Curtain.** One motif takes approximately 2¼ balls of Twilley's Lyscordet
**Edging.** One ball of Twilley's Lyscordet works approximately 17 ins of edging
One No.1·75 (ISR) crochet hook

**Note**
All rounds begin with 2tr in loop. This is worked as follows: 3ch, 1tr into loop last worked in previous round. This applies only to the first 2tr of each round. All rounds are joined with a ss.

## Motif

Using No.1·75 (ISR) hook make 6ch. Join with a ss into first ch to form circle.
**1st round** 3ch, 2tr into circle, 3ch, *3tr into circle, 3ch, rep from * twice. Join with a ss.
**2nd round** *2tr in loop, 1tr into each of next 3tr, into 3ch loop work 2tr, 3ch, rep from * 3 times. Join with a ss.
**3rd round** *2tr in loop, 1tr into each of next 3tr, into next tr work 4tr, take hook out of last st and insert it into first of 4tr, draw loop from fourth tr through first to form cluster—called 1cl—1tr into each of next 3tr, 2tr into 3ch loop, 3ch, rep from * 3 times. Join with a ss.
**4th round** *2tr in loop, 1tr into each of next 3tr, (1cl into next tr, 1tr into each of next 3tr) twice, 2tr into corner 3ch loop, 3ch, rep from * 3 times. Join with a ss.
**5th round** *2tr in loop, 3tr, (1cl, 3tr) 3 times, 2tr into corner 3ch loop, 3ch, rep from * 3 times.
**6th round** *2tr in loop, 3tr, (1cl, 3tr) 4 times, 2 tr into corner 3ch loop, 3ch, rep from * 3 times.
**7th round** *2tr in loop, 2tr, 8ch, 5tr, (1cl, 3tr) 3 times, 2tr, 8ch, 2tr, 2tr into corner 3ch loop, 3ch, rep from * 3 times.
**8th round** *2tr in loop, 2tr, 4ch, 1dc in 8ch loop, 4ch, miss 2tr, 5tr, (1cl, 3tr) twice, 2tr, 4ch, 1dc in 8ch loop, 4ch, miss 2tr, 2tr, 2tr into corner 3ch loop, 3ch, rep from * 3 times.
**9th round** *2tr in loop, 2tr, 4ch, 1dc in loop, 1dc in dc, 1dc in loop, 4ch, miss 2tr, 5tr, 1cl, 5tr, 4ch, 1dc in loop, 1dc in dc, 1dc in loop, 4ch, miss 2tr, 2tr, 2tr into corner 3ch loop, 3ch, rep from * 3 times.
**10th round** *2tr in loop, 2tr, 4ch, 1dc in loop, 3dc, 1dc in loop, 4ch, miss 2tr, 7tr, 4ch, 1dc in loop, 3dc, 1dc in loop,

4ch, miss 2tr, 2tr, 2tr into corner 3ch loop, 3ch, rep from * 3 times.
**11th round** *2tr in loop, 2tr, 4ch, 1dc in loop, 5dc, 1dc in loop, 4ch, miss 2tr, 3tr, 4ch, 1dc in loop, 5dc, 1dc in loop, 4ch, miss 2tr, 2tr, 2tr into corner 3ch loop, 3ch, rep from *3 times.
**12th round** *2tr in loop, 4tr, 2tr in next loop, 4ch, miss 1dc, 5dc, 4ch, 2tr in next loop, 3tr, 2tr in next loop, 4ch, miss 1dc, 5dc, 4ch, 2tr in next loop, 4tr, 2tr into corner 3ch loop, 3ch, rep from * 3 times.
**13th round** *2tr in loop, 8tr, 2tr in next loop, 4ch, miss 1dc, 3dc, 4ch, 2tr in next loop, 7tr, 2tr in next loop, 4ch, miss 1dc, 3dc, 4ch, 2tr in next loop, 8tr, 2tr into corner 3ch loop, 3ch, rep from * 3 times.
**14th round** *2tr in loop, 12tr, 2tr in next loop, 4ch, miss 1dc, 1dc, 4ch, 2tr in next loop, 11tr, 2tr in next loop, 4ch, miss 1dc, 1dc, 4ch, 2tr in next loop, 12tr, 2tr into corner 3ch loop, 3ch, rep from * 3 times.
**15th round** *2tr in loop, 16tr, 2tr in loop, 2tr in next loop, 15tr, 2tr in loop, 2tr in next loop, 16tr, 2tr into corner 3ch loop, 3ch, rep from * 3 times.
**16th round** *2tr in loop, (1 tr in next tr, 1ch, miss 1tr) 29 times, 1tr in last tr, 2tr into corner 3ch loop, 3ch, rep from * 3 times.
**17th round** *2tr in loop, 2tr, (1tr in tr, 1tr in ch) 29 times, 3tr, 2tr into corner 3ch loop, 3ch, rep from * 3 times.
**18th round** *2tr in loop, 3tr, (1cl, 3tr) 16 times, 2tr into corner 3ch loop, 3ch, rep from * 3 times.
**19th round** *2tr in loop, 3tr, (1cl, 3tr) 17 times, 2tr into corner 3ch loop, 3ch, rep from * 3 times.
**20th round** *2tr in loop, 1tr in each st to next corner, 2tr into corner 3ch loop, 3ch, rep from * 3 times.
**21st round** *2tr in loop, (1tr in next tr, 1ch, miss 1tr) 39 times, 1tr in last tr, 2tr into

corner 3ch loop, 3ch, rep from * 3 times.
**22nd round** *2tr in loop, 2tr, (1tr in tr, 1tr in ch) 39 times, 3tr, 2tr into corner 3ch loop, 3ch, rep from * 3 times.
**23rd round** *2tr in loop, 3tr, (1cl, 3tr) 6 times, 36tr, (1cl, 3tr) 6 times, 2tr into corner 3ch loop, 3ch, rep from * 3 times.
**24th round** *2tr in loop, 3tr, 1cl, (1ch, miss 1tr, 1tr in next tr) 9 times, 1ch, miss 1tr, 1cl, 21tr, 1cl, 21tr, 1cl, (1ch, miss 1tr, 1tr in next tr) 9 times, 1ch, miss 1tr, 1cl, 3tr, 2tr into corner 3ch loop, 3ch, rep from * 3 times.
**25th round** *2tr in loop, 3tr, 1cl, (1ch, miss 1ch, 1tr) 9 times, 1ch, 1cl in next tr, 21tr, 1cl, 3tr, 1cl, 21tr, 1cl, (1ch, miss 1tr, 1tr) 9 times, 1ch, 1cl, 3tr, 2tr into corner 3ch loop, 3ch, rep from * 3 times.
**26th round** *2tr in loop, 3tr, 1cl, (1ch, miss 1st, 1tr) 9 times, 1ch, miss 1st, 1cl, 21tr, 1cl, (1ch, miss 1st, 1tr) 3 times, 1ch, miss 1st, 1cl, 21tr, 1cl, (1ch, miss 1st, 1tr) 9 times, 1ch, miss 1st, 1cl, 3tr, 2tr into corner 3ch loop, 3ch, rep from * 3 times.
**27th round** *2tr in loop, 3tr, 1cl, (1ch, miss 1st, 1tr) 9 times, 1ch, miss 1st, 1cl, 21tr, 1cl, (1ch, miss 1st, 1tr) 5 times, 1ch, miss 1st, 1cl, 21tr, 1cl, (1ch, miss 1st, 1tr) 9 times, 1ch, miss 1st, 1cl, 3tr, 2tr into corner 3ch loop, 3ch, rep from * 3 times.
Finish off. Darn in all ends.

## Edging

Using No.1·75 (ISR) hook make 40ch.
**1st row** Insert hook into 5th ch from hook, 1dc, 2ch, miss 2ch, *1tr into each of next 2ch, 5tr into next ch, take hook out of last tr and insert into first of 5tr, draw through loop of 5th tr to form cluster—called large cl—1tr into each of next 2ch, 2ch, miss 2ch, 1dc into next ch, 2ch, miss 2ch, rep from * once, 1tr into each of next 15ch. Turn.

**2nd row** 2ch, 13tr between tr, 4ch, 1dc into next ch loop, * 4ch, 1dc into next ch loop, rep from * 3 times. Turn.

**3rd row** 4ch, 1dc into ch loop, 2ch, *work 2tr, 1 large cl, 2tr into next ch loop, 2ch, 1dc into next ch loop, 2ch, rep from * once, miss 2tr, 12tr between tr. Turn.

**4th row** 2ch, 10tr between tr, *4ch, 1dc into next ch loop, rep from * 4 times. Turn.

**5th row** 4ch, 1dc in loop, 2ch, *work 2tr, 1 large cl, 2tr into next ch loop, 2ch, 1dc into next loop, 2ch, rep from * once, miss 2tr, 9tr between tr. Turn.

**6th row** 2ch, 7tr between tr, *4ch, 1dc in next ch loop, rep from * 4 times. Turn.

**7th row** 4ch, 1dc in next loop, 2ch, *work 2tr, 1 large cl, 2tr in next loop, 2ch, 1dc in next loop, 2ch, rep from * once, 6 tr between tr. Turn.

**8th row** 2ch, 4tr between tr, * 4ch, 1dc in next loop, rep from * 4 times. Turn.

**9th row** 7ch, 1dc in next loop, 2ch, *work 2tr, 1 large cl, 2tr in next loop, 2ch, 1dc in next loop, 2ch, rep from * once, 3tr between tr. Turn.

**10th row** 2ch, 2tr between tr, 2tr in next loop, *4ch, 1dc in next loop, rep from * 4 times. Turn.

**11th row** 7ch, insert hook in 5th ch, 1dc, 2ch, *work 2tr, 1 large cl, 2tr in next loop, 2ch, 1dc in next loop, 2ch, rep from * once, 2tr in next loop, 4tr between tr. Turn.

**12th row** 2ch, 5tr between tr, 2tr in loop, *4ch, 1dc in next loop, rep from * 4 times. Turn.

**13th row** 7ch, 1dc in 5th of 7ch, 2ch, *work 2tr, 1 large cl, 2tr in next loop, 2ch, 1dc in next loop, 2ch, rep from * once, 2tr in loop, 7tr between tr. Turn.

**14th row** 2ch, 8tr between tr, 2tr in next loop, *4ch, 1dc in next loop, rep from * 4 times. Turn.

**15th row** 7ch, 1dc in 5th of 7ch, 2ch, *work 2tr, 1 large cl, 2tr in next loop, 2ch, 1dc

in next loop, 2ch, rep from * once, 2tr in next loop, 10tr between tr. Turn.

**16th row** 2ch, 11tr between tr, 2tr in next loop, *4ch, 1dc in next loop, rep from * 4 times. Turn.

Rep from 1st to 16th rows

for required length working 1st row as follows:
7ch, 1dc in 5th of 7ch, 2ch, *2tr, 1 large cl, 2tr in next loop, 2ch, 1dc in next loop, 2ch, rep from * once, 2tr in next loop, 13tr between tr. Turn.

## To make up

Press each motif and edging under a damp cloth.
Curtain shown here consists of 7 rows with 4 motifs in each row. Sew or crochet motifs tog, sew on edging.

# All about making Roman blinds

Roman blinds have great appeal; they look just like roller blinds when they are down over the window, but have a soft, folded look when they are pulled up and take the place of a pelmet. The directions given here are easy to follow, provided you so do carefully and have the right tools and parts for the job. Alternative finishes are given for the top and bottom of the blind, and there are three different methods of attaching the blind at the window.

### Suitable fabrics
**Cover fabric.** Furnishing fabrics like ticking, cotton, linen and man-made fibre mixtures are all suitable for Roman blinds, provided they are not too thick. Dress fabrics are not guaranteed fade proof and are therefore only suitable for windows which are not subject to direct sunlight.
**Lining fabric.** To line Roman blinds, use cotton sateen as for unlined curtains. If you plan to use coloured sateen, dye the tapes to match.

### Measuring up
Figures 1, 2 and 3 show three methods of fixing the blind, two of which are batten fixings and one a pole fixing.

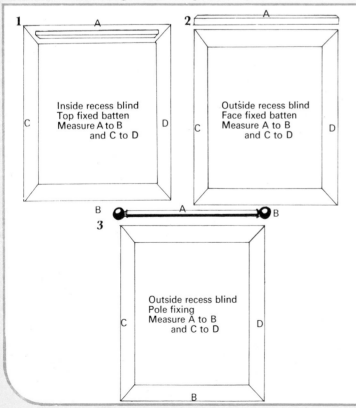

*The Roman blinds used in this traditionally elegant room add to the grace of*

Decide which method you wish to use and then measure the window as shown in the respective diagram.
Measurement A to B is the drop from where the blind will start to where it will end. Add at least 10 inches for turnings, making pockets and neatening.
Measurement C to D is the width of the blind.
If you are using an inside recess fitting, measure the width of the recess and deduct 1 to 1½ inches on each side to allow the blind room to move up and down. Add 2 inches for turnings.
If you are using an outside recess fitting, measure the width of the window and add 2 inches turning allowance as before. But if you want the blind to keep out more light, add a further 1½ inches at each side.

### The parts of a Roman blind
Figure 4 shows the wrong side of a finished blind. The different parts are labelled and the measurements given between the rings and tapes will help you to estimate how much tape, how many rings, vine eyes or china thimbles and how much nylon cord to buy. Figure 5 shows the different parts of the blind in detail.
**The 2in by 1in wooden batten.** This holds the blind at the top

*ws. The soft folds of the raised blinds take the place of pelmets*

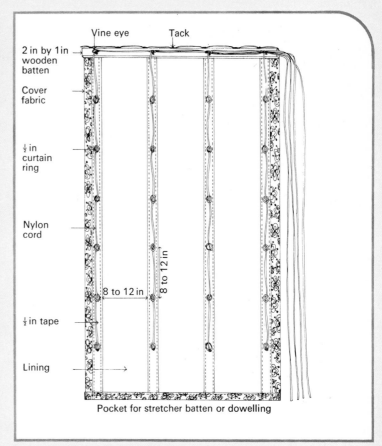

▲ **4.** *Wrong side of a finished blind*   ▼ **5.** *The parts of a Roman blind*

Diagram 4 labels:
Vine eye  Tack
2 in by 1 in wooden batten
Cover fabric
½ in curtain ring
Nylon cord
8 to 12 in   8 to 12 in
8 to 12 in
½ in tape
Lining
Pocket for stretcher batten or dowelling

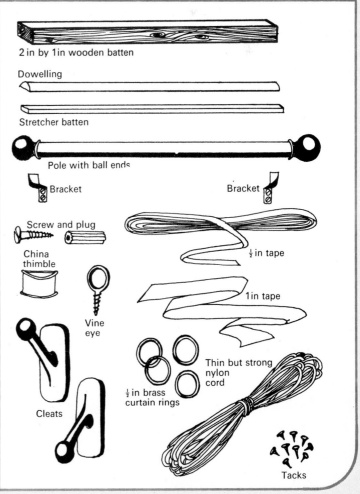

Diagram 5 labels:
2 in by 1 in wooden batten
Dowelling
Stretcher batten
Pole with ball ends
Bracket    Bracket
Screw and plug
China thimble
Vine eye
Cleats
½ in tape
1 in tape
½ in brass curtain rings
Thin but strong nylon cord
Tacks

and takes the vine eyes or china thimbles. The batten is screwed into the wall or recess above the window.

**The pole, ball ends and brackets.** These are used instead of the batten if you want a pole fixing.

**The vine eyes or china thimbles.** These are screwed into the batten or pole to take the cords at the top of the blind, and are spaced evenly at 8 to 12 inch intervals (whichever measurement divides most closely into the width of the blind).

**The ½ inch tapes.** These are stitched to the blind, spaced evenly at 8 to 12 inch intervals as before.

**The ½ inch rings.** These are stitched to the tapes, spaced evenly at 8 to 12 inch intervals (whichever divides most closely into the length of the blind).

**The nylon cords.** These run from the lowest ring to the top ring on each tape, through the vine eyes or china thimbles on the batten or pole, and reach down to at least the length of the blind.

**The cleats.** These hold the cords when the blind is pulled up.

**The stretcher batten or dowelling.** This stabilises and gives weight to the bottom of the blind.

**The 1 inch tape.** This takes the tacks which hold the blind to a face fixed batten, so that the tacks are hidden.

**▲ 6.** *Lining tacked to the cover*
**9.** *1 inch tape stitched to the blind* ▶
**▼ 8.** *Blind top fixed to a batten*

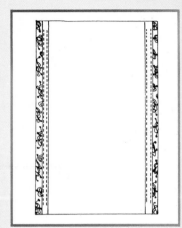

**▲ 7.** *Tapes machined into place*

**▼ 10.** *1 inch tape cross stitched*

Tack

Batten →

Vine eye →

Lining ——— → Cover

← Pocket for
stretcher batten

**▼11.***Vine eyes in position on a pole*

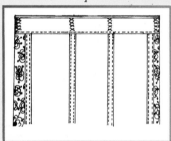

**▼ 12.** *Threading first line of rings*

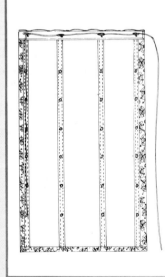

## You will need

For batten fixing:
- ☐ 2in by 1in wooden batten as long as the width of the finished blind
- ☐ Tacks
- ☐ 1in wide straight tape (for a face fixed batten only)

For a pole fixing:
- ☐ A wooden pole, a little longer than the width of the finished blind, ball ends and brackets

For both types of fixings:
- ☐ Cover fabric
- ☐ Lining fabric
- ☐ Matching sewing thread, tacking cotton
- ☐ Vine eyes or china thimbles
- ☐ $\frac{1}{2}$in curtain rings
- ☐ 2 cleats
- ☐ Thin but strong nylon cord
- ☐ $\frac{1}{2}$in wide tape
- ☐ 1in stretcher batten, or dowelling, cut to the width of the finished blind
- ☐ A screw driver, screws and plugs
- ☐ A hammer

## Cutting out
**Fabric.** Cut the cover fabric for the blind to the required measurements.
Make sure that the corners of the fabric are square by checking them with a set square, or against the corner of a table.
Cut the lining fabric in the same way.
**Tapes.** Cut the $\frac{1}{2}$ inch tape into as many lengths, each equal to the length of the blind fabric, as you will need.
If you are using a face fixed batten, trim the length of 1 inch tape to the same width as the blind fabric.

## Making up
Fold in the sides of the cover fabric 1 inch. Fold in the sides of the lining fabric 1½ inches, press all the turned edges.
Place the turned lining over the turned cover, wrong sides facing, so that the folded edges of the lining are $\frac{1}{2}$ inch from each folded edge of the cover.
Tack the lining to the cover (figure 6).
Place a length of $\frac{1}{2}$ inch tape over each edge of the lining and tack into position. Machine down both sides of each tape, thus holding the lining, tape and cover fabric in place as shown in figure 7.
Leave $\frac{3}{4}$ inch of tape unstitched at each end.
Stitch the remainder of the tapes into position (see figure 4), leaving $\frac{3}{4}$ inch unstitched at both ends of each tape.
Neaten the top and bottom of the blind by turning under $\frac{3}{8}$ inch on both lining and cover, and slip stitching along the turned edges (the tapes will be turned under with the lining).

## Finishing at the bottom of the blind
Turn up the bottom edge of the blind to make a pocket for the stretcher batten or dowelling. Machine stitch the turned edge down and slip the stretcher batten or dowelling into place. Hand-sew each end of the pocket to close.

## Finishing the top of the blind
**For a top fixed batten.** The top edge of the blind is held with tacks over the top of the batten (figure 8).
**For a pole.** Turn over enough of the top edge of the blind to make a pocket for the pole, and make a pocket as for the stretcher batten, but do not close the ends. Slip the pole into the pocket and screw on the ball ends.
**For a face fixed batten.** Take the length of 1 inch tape and turn under the ends for 1 inch to neaten them. Stitch the tape onto the lining side of the blind so that the top edge of the tape lines up with the top edge of the blind (figure 9).
Using a cross stitch, hand-sew the tape to the lining at 8 to 12 inch intervals (figure 10). This forms pockets in the tape in which the tacks will be placed. Tack the blind onto the face of the batten through the tape so that the tacks do not show on the right side of the blind. The cross stitching will prevent the top edge of the blind from sagging.

▲ *Striking simplicity in a modern setting. The contrasting borders on these beautifully proportioned Roman blinds echo the clear lines of the windows*

## Stitching on the rings
The rings should be set onto the tapes 8 to 12 inches away from the top and bottom of the blind, and spaced evenly no less than 8 inches and no more than 12 inches apart. Sew them on with double cotton to hold them firmly (see figure 4).

## Fixing the vine eyes or china thimbles
**Batten fixing.** Vine eyes or china thimbles are screwed into the underside of the batten at the same intervals as the tapes (see figure 4).
**Pole fixing.** The vine eyes are screwed into the back of the pole, through the blind fabric, at the same intervals as the tapes (figure 11).

## Threading the rings
First, decide on which side of the window you want the cleats.
If the cleats are to be on the right side then start threading from the ring in the bottom left hand corner. If the cleats are to be on the left then start from the bottom right hand corner.
Lay the blind flat and tie and then sew the end of the cord to the starting ring. Thread the cord through all the rings on the first tape and then through the vine eye or china thimble at the top of the tape. Continue threading the cord through all the vine eyes or china thimbles to the right (or left) of the first, take the cord to the bottom of the blind and cut it off (figure 12).

Thread the next row of rings in this way and continue until all the rings are threaded (see figure 4).
Gather the ends of the cords together and knot them so that all the cords work together and pull up the folds in unison.

## Dressing the blind
Pull the cords so that the blind is folded, and leave it folded for at least 24 hours. This helps the blind to hang and fold better when it is finally in position.

## Hanging the blind
Mark the spots where the screws are to be inserted to hold the batten or pole in position.
For the batten, drill holes both in the batten and the wall or recess. Screw the batten firmly into position using plugs to fix the screws.
For the pole, screw the brackets into position, and mount the pole on the brackets.

## Fixing the cleats
At whichever side of the window you have decided to position the cleats, fix them in pairs, one above the other, with the peg of the top cleat pointing up and the peg of the bottom cleat pointing down.
The bottom cleat should be just above the level of the sill and the top cleat 10 to 12 inches above this.

# A variation of shades

Both of the pretty lampshades in this chapter are made on the basic Tiffany shape and each one could be completed in a single evening.

## You will need
- [ ] Hemispherical Tiffany lampshade 10 inches in diameter
- [ ] 1 roll white bias binding
- [ ] $\frac{1}{2}$ yard elastic
- [ ] $\frac{1}{2}$ yard straight tape
- [ ] Small tin white lacquer (optional)
- [ ] For the fringed shade—$\frac{1}{2}$ yard broderie Anglaise fabric 36 inches wide and 1 yard fringing
- [ ] or for the scalloped shade—$\frac{1}{2}$ yard printed lawn 36 inches wide

## Preparing the frame
If the lampshade frame is not already covered in plastic or painted it must be lacquered to prevent rusting. The frame must then be bound to protect the lampshade covering from the hard edges of the frame. Bias binding should be used as it can be wound more tightly round the struts than straight binding.

Starting at the top of one of the side struts (figure 1), loop the binding round the 'T' joint (figure 2).

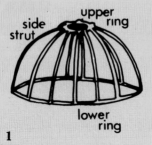
1

2

Bind firmly round and round the strut, continuing downwards to the lower ring. Secure the binding by looping back the end under one of the coils and pulling it taut (figure 3). Sew the free end to the bound strut with tiny stitches.

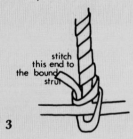
3

Bind all the side struts in this way and then the upper and lower rings.

## The fringed shade
Cut a strip of broderie Anglaise fabric 33 inches long by 11 inches wide. Fold it in half, wrong sides together, and make a French seam along the 11 inch side (figure 4). This tube

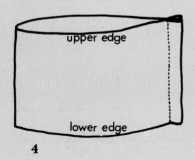
4

of fabric should now slip over the frame and fit the frame at its widest part.

Turn the raw upper edge of the fabric over a $\frac{1}{4}$ inch and then turn the fabric again to make a $\frac{1}{2}$ inch hem. Stitch the hem, leaving a 1 inch opening. Do the same with the lower edge of the tube.

Turn the fabric right side out and stitch the fringing on to it, 1 inch from the lower edge (figure 5).

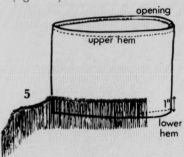
5

Insert the elastic through the opening in the lower hem and secure it so that when the tube of fabric is pulled over the frame the lower hem is drawn inside the bottom ring of the frame (figure 6). Insert the

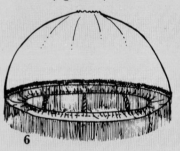
6

straight tape into the upper hem through the opening. Pull up the tape until the tube of fabric fits over the shade fairly tightly and the fringe lies around the lower ring of the frame. Tie the straight tape and neaten the ends.

## Scalloped shade
First make a tube of lawn as explained for the fringed shade. To make scallops cut another strip of lawn 33 inches long, but only 6 inches wide. Fold it in half, right sides together, and make a $\frac{1}{2}$ inch plain seam along the 6 inch side (figure 7). Press the seam open. Fold this tube of fabric in half lengthways and tack the raw edges together (figure 8).

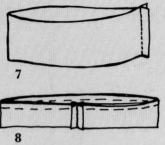
7

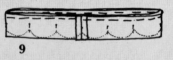
8

Mark this tube of fabric into 12 equal sections with pins placed 1 inch from the folded edge. Using a suitable circular article as a template (a tin or a glass) draw in the scallops with a pencil. Machine stitch along the line of scallops (figure 9).

9

Trim and snip carefully between the scallops and turn right side out. Press carefully. The scalloped tube should now look like figure 10.

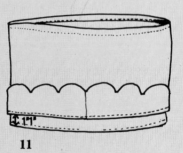
10

Stitch the scalloped tube on to the hemmed tube which you have already made, 1 inch from the lower edge (figure 11).

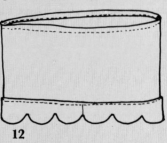
11

Turn the scallops down over the lower part of the shade and machine stitch $\frac{1}{4}$ inch from the previous join (figure 12). Insert

the elastic and tape, and mount the shade on to the frame following the instructions for the fringed lampshade.

# Blooming wall panels

These delightful Art Deco flowers bring a modern look to canvas work and are something you could design yourself. By changing the colour scheme you can completely change the mood of the panel, using bright, clear colours for summer flowers, as in the summer flowers panel on the opposite page, or rusty yellows and oranges for the autumn ones below.

▼ *This wall panel depicts flowers in the mellow tones of autumn*

Apart from single and double weave canvas you can also use many canvas work stitches on softer cotton or jute cloths with Aida weaves. True Aida cloth is a cotton embroidery fabric woven in blocks of threads. It has a slightly starched finish which launders out once the embroidery is completed. This cloth is too fine for standard canvas work wools but the jute canvas with Aida weave, which comes in one size only, gives six cross stitches to the inch. This produces quick results and these bold wall panels can be worked in just a few hours. Alternatively, use Binca cloth which is similar.

## Summer flowers panel

### Materials you will need
☐ ½yd Aida weave jute canvas (finished size about 15in square)
☐ Tapestry needle size 18
☐ Hardboard or softboard 15in by 15in
☐ 1 skein white, 3 skeins orange, 3 skeins blue, 1 skein brown, 9 skeins pink, 2 skeins yellow, 6 skeins green, 12 skeins turquoise (background)

**NB** You can use either soft embroidery cotton or tapisserie wool. The amounts given above are for tapisserie wool which has 15 yards to the skein, whereas soft embroidery cotton skeins contain 10 yards. Allowing for an equivalent yardage, in some cases more skeins of soft embroidery cotton will be required. Use one strand throughout.

### To work the picture
First find the centre of the canvas by working two lines of tacking, one from side to side and one from top to bottom as indicated by the arrows on the chart (page 82). Work the design by counting out from the centre of the chart, outlining the shapes in back stitch first then fill in the design with cross stitch. Each cross stitch is worked following the weave of the canvas, which is divided into squares.

### To mount the finished work
When the design is completed, you should stretch the canvas to prevent it puckering. Trim the board to the exact finished size of the panel. Lay the board centrally over the back of the work and lace the canvas with fine string, picking up the fabric well in from the edge. Take the lacing across the back from side to side and then repeat the process from top to bottom. Pull the lacing firmly so that the work is evenly stretched without puckering. Secure the ends of the string by knotting them several times.
If you want to hang the panel unframed, make the work neat by sewing unbleached calico or holland over the back to conceal the lacing.

## Autumn flowers panel

### Designing your own picture
To design a flower picture such as the one shown here, working on stiff paper, simply draw round drinking glasses to form the flower shapes. Cut out several flowers in varying sizes and then arrange them, overlapping, until you achieve a pleasing effect. Trace the outline of the design on to the canvas and work in cross stitch as for the summer flowers.

### Larger scale canvas work
To work to an even larger scale use rug wools or two strands of double knitting wool on continental jute, which is made for rugs and has a similar weave to Aida cloth, which will give 4 cross stitches to the inch. Worked on this larger scale canvas, the summer flowers panel will measure about 22 inches square.

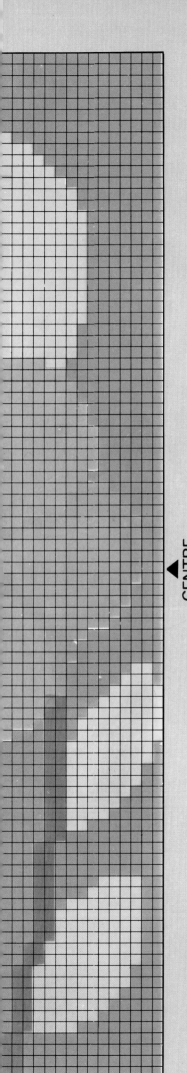

◀ CENTRE

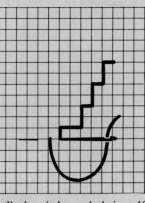

▲ *Back stitch worked in self colour to outline shapes.*

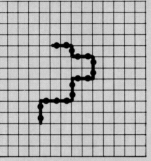

▲ *Back stitch worked in contrast colour indicated on the chart*

# Stitch Library

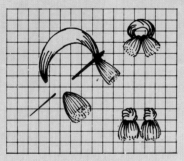

### Single or tufted stitch
*The stitches are worked between each other in alternate rows and imitate carpet knotting*

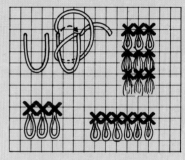

### Velvet or astrakhan stitch
*All the stitches should be worked before any of the loops are cut*

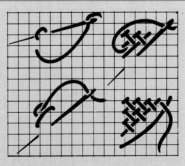

### Web stitch
*Web stitch gives a woven effect and is useful as a filling for small areas*

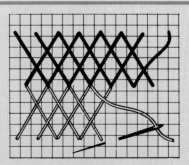

### Plaited Algerian stitch
*This is worked in the same way as closed herringbone stitch*

# Covering a stool in canvas work

If a favourite stool shows signs of wear on the top fabric, it is a relatively simple matter to work a new top in canvas work to re-cover it. The stitches shown in this chapter suggest stripes which make a colourful topping for stools.

Canvas work is particularly suitable for stool tops because it is so hard wearing. For the best results the important thing to bear in mind is always to use the best quality yarns and linen canvas. Also, special care must be taken when planning the design as this must view equally well from every angle. The stitches shown on these pages suggest stripes, which can be most attractive when worked in carefully selected colours.

## Materials you will need
☐ Linen canvas (to assess the amount required measure across the width of the stool top plus the drop on both sides. Measure in the same way for the length and add 6 inches to each measurement to allow for stretching)
☐ Muslin of a similar amount
☐ Soft lead pencil
☐ Dressmaking pins
☐ Tapisserie wool or crewel wool in the amounts specified for the design chosen
☐ Tapestry needle No.18
☐ Fine ½in upholstery tacks for corners
☐ Brass headed upholstery tacks (sufficient to go round the stool placed closely together)

## Before you begin
Remove the old covering and make sure that the existing padding is firm and even. If not, the top should be re-upholstered.

## Making a pattern
Working out the shape of the pattern is first done with muslin, just like a toile in dressmaking. The muslin must be big enough to more than cover the seat area and the drop. Using a soft pencil, mark a vertical and horizontal line from side to side across the centre of the muslin, using the thread of the weave as a guide. Draw similar centre lines on the stool. Position the muslin on the stool, matching the lines. Pin the muslin to the stool top, starting at the centre of the crossed lines and working out simultaneously to all four sides, placing the pins at 3 inch intervals. Continue these lines of pins down the depth of the drop. Pin the corners to make mitres.

With a soft pencil, mark the area of the top of the stool, the edge of the frame and both sides of each mitred corner. Take the muslin off the stool and measure the length and width of the muslin to make sure that it corresponds exactly to the measurements of the stool. If it does not, the muslin has been pulled out of shape. Working on a firm surface, pin the muslin onto brown paper, making sure that the weave of the muslin is straight. The pattern on the muslin may be slightly irregular but make the brown paper pattern absolutely symmetrical. Mark the vertical

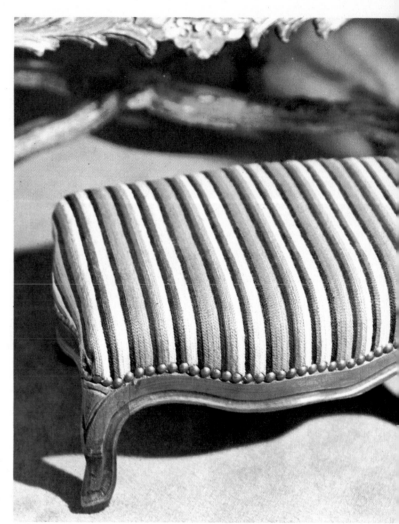

▲ *An example of a stool top worked in stripes of chain stitch*

and horizontal lines on the canvas to match up with those on the paper pattern. Pin the pattern to the canvas and mark with a felt pen round the edge. This gives the area of the canvas to be worked. Cut the canvas to a square leaving at least a 3 inch margin all round for stretching.

## Covering the stool
When you have completed stitching the design on the canvas for the stool cover, stretch and trim the work to prevent it from puckering, and remember to leave the unworked areas of canvas in the corners for mitring. Turn the seam allowances to the back of the work and secure with tacking thread.

Fit the cover over the stool, matching the centre lines, and hammer in a brass headed tack at each of the four points where these lines end. Cover

the head of the hammer with a duster to prevent damage to the tacks.

Smooth the canvas out from two of these centre points on adjacent sides, working towards the corner and tacking with brass headed tacks as you go. Fix the point of the canvas corner to the stool using an upholstery tack and then ease the edges of the worked canvas together to meet at the corner edge (see diagram).

Work the remaining corners in the same way, working the diagonally opposite corner next.

## Working the canvas
**Chain stitch method 1.** This is a very quick method worked with a fine crochet hook, missing two holes of the canvas with each stitch. For a shorter stitch miss one hole each time, for a longer one, miss more. Do not make the stitches too long or the work will wear

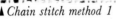
▲ *Chain stitch method 1*

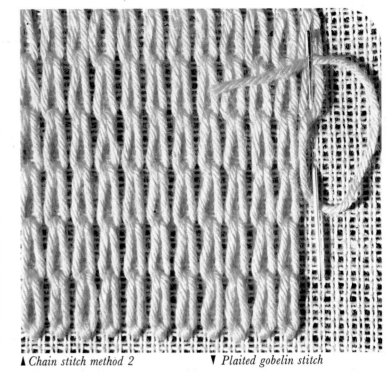
▲ *Chain stitch method 2*    ▼ *Plaited gobelin stitch*

badly. When one row is completed, finish off and start the next unless continuing in the same colour, in which case turn the work and commence the next row. It is essential to finish ends securely because if they work loose a whole row of stitching will come undone.

**Chain stitch method 2.** Work this like ordinary chain stitch as shown in the illustration. Finish the end of each row with a small stitch to hold the last chain in place. Once again, finish off the end of the thread securely.

**Plaited Gobelin.** This stitch is worked in horizontal rows over four threads up and two across to the left. Work to the length of the area you want to cover leaving a space of two threads between each stitch. The second row is worked two threads down and in the opposite direction, giving a plaited or woven effect.

▼ *Pinning muslin toile onto stool*    ▼ *Pattern shape pinned to canvas*    ▼ *Fitting the corner of the canvas*

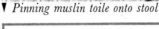

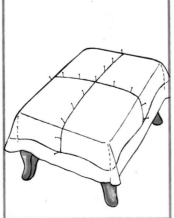

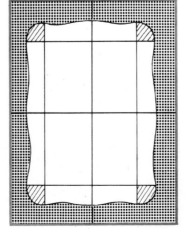

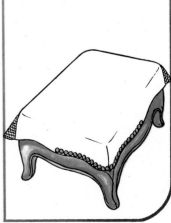

# Design from a tile in quick point

Adapted from a tile patterned wall paper, this striking design in chunky yarns is quick to work. The stitch used here is half cross stitch but other stitches can be used to create more textured effects. Several exciting ideas for using the design are illustrated and similar designs can be lifted from pottery tiles.

To work the panel measuring 18 inches square you will need:
- [ ] Piece of single weave canvas 24 inches square with 21 threads to 2 inches
- [ ] Piece of lining fabric measuring 20 inches square
- [ ] Piece of 1 ply wood cut to measure 18 inches square for mounting
- [ ] Tapestry needle size 18
- [ ] DMC Art 313 Embroidery Wool in the following colours and amounts: 7 skeins blue 7317; 6 skeins blue 7313; 5 skeins blue 7314; 1 skein blue 7307; 4 skeins green 7351; 2 skeins green 7346; 1 skein green 7428; 5 skeins white

## To work the panel

Work the panel in half cross stitch over one thread of the canvas. Stretch completed work and mount the panel over the wood. Finish the edges with a finger knotted cord and four large tassels. Make a further length of finger knotted cord to hang the panel.

▼ *This chart shows ¼ of the design. Each square = 1 stitch*

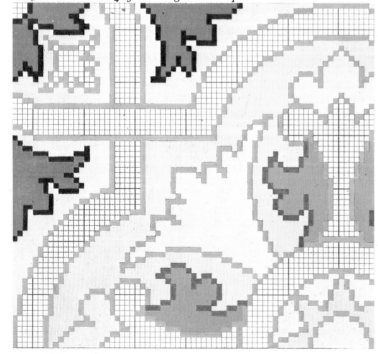